HOSNI MUBARAK

HOSNI MUBARAK

John Solecki

CHELSEA HOUSE PUBLISHERS
NEW YORK
PHILADELPHIA

Chelsea House Publishers

EDITOR-IN-CHIEF: Remmel Nunn
MANAGING EDITOR: Karyn Gullen Browne
COPY CHIEF: Juliann Barbato
PICTURE EDITOR: Adrian G. Allen
ART DIRECTOR: Maria Epes
DEPUTY COPY CHIEF: Mark Rifkin
ASSISTANT ART DIRECTOR: Loraine Machlin
MANUFACTURING MANAGER: Gerald Levine
SYSTEMS MANAGER: Rachel Vigier
PRODUCTION MANAGER: Joseph Romano
PRODUCTION COORDINATOR: Marie Claire Cebrián

World Leaders—Past & Present

SENIOR EDITOR: John W. Selfridge

Staff for HOSNI MUBARAK

ASSOCIATE EDITOR: Jeff Klein
COPY EDITOR: Brian Sookram
EDITORIAL ASSISTANT: Martin Mooney
PICTURE RESEARCHER: Nisa Rauschenberg
DESIGNER: David Murray
DESIGN ASSISTANT: Diana Blume
COVER ILLUSTRATION: Bill Donahey

First Printing

1 3 5 7 9 8 6 4 2

Library of Congress Cataloging-in-Publication Data

Solecki, John.
  Hosni Mubarak/John Solecki.
  p.   cm.—(World leaders—past and present)
  Includes bibliographical references and index.
  Summary: A biography of the current president of Egypt.
  ISBN 1-55546-844-6
        0-7910-0681-6 (pbk.)
  1. Mubārak, Muhammad Husni, 1928–   —Juvenile literature.
2. Presidents—Egypt—Biography—Juvenile literature. [1. Mubārak,
Muhammad Husnī, 1928–   . 2. Presidents—Egypt.] I. Title.
II. Series: World leaders past & present.
DT107.823.M82S65   1990
962.05′5′092—dc20   90–35962
[B]   CIP
[92]   AC

Contents

John Adams
John Quincy Adams
Konrad Adenauer
Alexander the Great
Salvador Allende
Marc Antony
Corazon Aquino
Yasir Arafat
King Arthur
Hafez al-Assad
Kemal Atatürk
Attila
Clement Attlee
Augustus Caesar
Menachem Begin
David Ben-Gurion
Otto von Bismarck
Léon Blum
Simon Bolívar
Cesare Borgia
Willy Brandt
Leonid Brezhnev
Julius Caesar
John Calvin
Jimmy Carter
Fidel Castro
Catherine the Great
Charlemagne
Chiang Kai-Shek
Winston Churchill
Georges Clemenceau
Cleopatra
Constantine the Great
Hernán Cortés
Oliver Cromwell
Georges-Jacques
   Danton
Jefferson Davis
Moshe Dayan
Charles de Gaulle
Eamon De Valera
Eugene Debs
Deng Xiaoping
Benjamin Disraeli
Alexander Dubček
François & Jean-Claude
   Duvalier
Dwight Eisenhower
Eleanor of Aquitaine
Elizabeth I
Faisal
Ferdinand & Isabella
Francisco Franco
Benjamin Franklin

Frederick the Great
Indira Gandhi
Mohandas Gandhi
Giuseppe Garibaldi
Amin & Bashir Gemayel
Genghis Khan
William Gladstone
Mikhail Gorbachev
Ulysses S. Grant
Ernesto "Che" Guevara
Tenzin Gyatso
Alexander Hamilton
Dag Hammarskjöld
Henry VIII
Henry of Navarre
Paul von Hindenburg
Hirohito
Adolf Hitler
Ho Chi Minh
King Hussein
Ivan the Terrible
Andrew Jackson
James I
Wojciech Jaruzelski
Thomas Jefferson
Joan of Arc
Pope John XXIII
Pope John Paul II
Lyndon Johnson
Benito Juárez
John Kennedy
Robert Kennedy
Jomo Kenyatta
Ayatollah Khomeini
Nikita Khrushchev
Kim Il Sung
Martin Luther King, Jr.
Henry Kissinger
Kublai Khan
Lafayette
Robert E. Lee
Vladimir Lenin
Abraham Lincoln
David Lloyd George
Louis XIV
Martin Luther
Judas Maccabeus
James Madison
Nelson & Winnie
   Mandela
Mao Zedong
Ferdinand Marcos
George Marshall

Mary, Queen of Scots
Tomáš Masaryk
Golda Meir
Klemens von Metternich
James Monroe
Hosni Mubarak
Robert Mugabe
Benito Mussolini
Napoléon Bonaparte
Gamal Abdel Nasser
Jawaharlal Nehru
Nero
Nicholas II
Richard Nixon
Kwame Nkrumah
Daniel Ortega
Mohammed Reza Pahlavi
Thomas Paine
Charles Stewart
   Parnell
Pericles
Juan Perón
Peter the Great
Pol Pot
Muammar el-Qaddafi
Ronald Reagan
Cardinal Richelieu
Maximilien Robespierre
Eleanor Roosevelt
Franklin Roosevelt
Theodore Roosevelt
Anwar Sadat
Haile Selassie
Prince Sihanouk
Jan Smuts
Joseph Stalin
Sukarno
Sun Yat-sen
Tamerlane
Mother Teresa
Margaret Thatcher
Josip Broz Tito
Toussaint L'Ouverture
Leon Trotsky
Pierre Trudeau
Harry Truman
Queen Victoria
Lech Walesa
George Washington
Chaim Weizmann
Woodrow Wilson
Xerxes
Emiliano Zapata
Zhou Enlai

ON LEADERSHIP

Arthur M. Schlesinger, jr.

LEADERSHIP, it may be said, is really what makes the world go round. Love no doubt smooths the passage; but love is a private transaction between consenting adults. Leadership is a public transaction with history. The idea of leadership affirms the capacity of individuals to move, inspire, and mobilize masses of people so that they act together in pursuit of an end. Sometimes leadership serves good purposes, sometimes bad; but whether the end is benign or evil, great leaders are those men and women who leave their personal stamp on history.

Now, the very concept of leadership implies the proposition that individuals can make a difference. This proposition has never been universally accepted. From classical times to the present day, eminent thinkers have regarded individuals as no more than the agents and pawns of larger forces, whether the gods and goddesses of the ancient world or, in the modern era, race, class, nation, the dialectic, the will of the people, the spirit of the times, history itself. Against such forces, the individual dwindles into insignificance.

So contends the thesis of historical determinism. Tolstoy's great novel *War and Peace* offers a famous statement of the case. Why, Tolstoy asked, did millions of men in the Napoleonic Wars, denying their human feelings and their common sense, move back and forth across Europe slaughtering their fellows? "The war," Tolstoy answered, "was bound to happen simply because it was bound to happen." All prior history predetermined it. As for leaders, they, Tolstoy said, "are but the labels that serve to give a name to an end and, like labels, they have the least possible connection with the event." The greater the leader, "the more conspicuous the inevitability and the predestination of every act he commits." The leader, said Tolstoy, is "the slave of history."

Determinism takes many forms. Marxism is the determinism of class. Nazism the determinism of race. But the idea of men and women as the slaves of history runs athwart the deepest human instincts. Rigid determinism abolishes the idea of human freedom—

the assumption of free choice that underlies every move we make, every word we speak, every thought we think. It abolishes the idea of human responsibility, since it is manifestly unfair to reward or punish people for actions that are by definition beyond their control. No one can live consistently by any deterministic creed. The Marxist states prove this themselves by their extreme susceptibility to the cult of leadership.

More than that, history refutes the idea that individuals make no difference. In December 1931 a British politician crossing Park Avenue in New York City between 76th and 77th Streets around 10:30 P.M. looked in the wrong direction and was knocked down by an automobile—a moment, he later recalled, of a man aghast, a world aglare: "I do not understand why I was not broken like an eggshell or squashed like a gooseberry." Fourteen months later an American politician, sitting in an open car in Miami, Florida, was fired on by an assassin; the man beside him was hit. Those who believe that individuals make no difference to history might well ponder whether the next two decades would have been the same had Mario Constasino's car killed Winston Churchill in 1931 and Giuseppe Zangara's bullet killed Franklin Roosevelt in 1933. Suppose, in addition, that Adolf Hitler had been killed in the street fighting during the Munich *Putsch* of 1923 and that Lenin had died of typhus during World War I. What would the 20th century be like now?

For better or for worse, individuals do make a difference. "The notion that a people can run itself and its affairs anonymously," wrote the philosopher William James, "is now well known to be the silliest of absurdities. Mankind does nothing save through initiatives on the part of inventors, great or small, and imitation by the rest of us—these are the sole factors in human progress. Individuals of genius show the way, and set the patterns, which common people then adopt and follow."

Leadership, James suggests, means leadership in thought as well as in action. In the long run, leaders in thought may well make the greater difference to the world. But, as Woodrow Wilson once said, "Those only are leaders of men, in the general eye, who lead in action. . . . It is at their hands that new thought gets its translation into the crude language of deeds." Leaders in thought often invent in solitude and obscurity, leaving to later generations the tasks of imitation. Leaders in action—the leaders portrayed in this series—have to be effective in their own time.

And they cannot be effective by themselves. They must act in response to the rhythms of their age. Their genius must be adapted, in a phrase of William James's, "to the receptivities of the moment." Leaders are useless without followers. "There goes the mob," said the French politician hearing a clamor in the streets. "I am their leader. I must follow them." Great leaders turn the inchoate emotions of the mob to purposes of their own. They seize on the opportunities of their time, the hopes, fears, frustrations, crises, potentialities. They succeed when events have prepared the way for them, when the community is awaiting to be aroused, when they can provide the clarifying and organizing ideas. Leadership ignites the circuit between the individual and the mass and thereby alters history.

It may alter history for better or for worse. Leaders have been responsible for the most extravagant follies and most monstrous crimes that have beset suffering humanity. They have also been vital in such gains as humanity has made in individual freedom, religious and racial tolerance, social justice, and respect for human rights.

There is no sure way to tell in advance who is going to lead for good and who for evil. But a glance at the gallery of men and women in *World Leaders—Past and Present* suggests some useful tests.

One test is this: Do leaders lead by force or by persuasion? By command or by consent? Through most of history leadership was exercised by the divine right of authority. The duty of followers was to defer and to obey. "Theirs not to reason why / Theirs but to do and die." On occasion, as with the so-called enlightened despots of the 18th century in Europe, absolutist leadership was animated by humane purposes. More often, absolutism nourished the passion for domination, land, gold, and conquest and resulted in tyranny.

The great revolution of modern times has been the revolution of equality. The idea that all people should be equal in their legal condition has undermined the old structure of authority, hierarchy, and deference. The revolution of equality has had two contrary effects on the nature of leadership. For equality, as Alexis de Tocqueville pointed out in his great study *Democracy in America*, might mean equality in servitude as well as equality in freedom.

"I know of only two methods of establishing equality in the political world," Tocqueville wrote. "Rights must be given to every citizen, or none at all to anyone . . . save one, who is the master of all." There was no middle ground "between the sovereignty of all and the absolute power of one man." In his astonishing prediction of 20th-century totalitarian dictatorship, Tocqueville explained how the revolution of equality could lead to the *"Führerprinzip"* and more terrible absolutism than the world had ever known.

But when rights are given to every citizen and the sovereignty of all is established, the problem of leadership takes a new form, becomes more exacting than ever before. It is easy to issue commands and enforce them by the rope and the stake, the concentration camp and the *gulag.* It is much harder to use argument and achievement to overcome opposition and win consent. The Founding Fathers of the United States understood the difficulty. They believed that history had given them the opportunity to decide, as Alexander Hamilton wrote in the first Federalist Paper, whether men are indeed capable of basing government on "reflection and choice, or whether they are forever destined to depend . . . on accident and force."

Government by reflection and choice called for a new style of leadership and a new quality of followership. It required leaders to be responsive to popular concerns, and it required followers to be active and informed participants in the process. Democracy does not eliminate emotion from politics; sometimes it fosters demagoguery; but it is confident that, as the greatest of democratic leaders put it, you cannot fool all of the people all of the time. It measures leadership by results and retires those who overreach or falter or fail.

It is true that in the long run despots are measured by results too. But they can postpone the day of judgment, sometimes indefinitely, and in the meantime they can do infinite harm. It is also true that democracy is no guarantee of virtue and intelligence in government, for the voice of the people is not necessarily the voice of God. But democracy, by assuring the right of opposition, offers built-in resistance to the evils inherent in absolutism. As the theologian Reinhold Niebuhr summed it up, "Man's capacity for justice makes democracy possible, but man's inclination to injustice makes democracy necessary."

A second test for leadership is the end for which power is sought. When leaders have as their goal the supremacy of a master race or the promotion of totalitarian revolution or the acquisition and exploitation of colonies or the protection of greed and privilege or the preservation of personal power, it is likely that their leadership will do little to advance the cause of humanity. When their goal is the abolition of slavery, the liberation of women, the enlargement of opportunity for the poor and powerless, the extension of equal rights to racial minorities, the defense of the freedoms of expression and opposition, it is likely that their leadership will increase the sum of human liberty and welfare.

Leaders have done great harm to the world. They have also conferred great benefits. You will find both sorts in this series. Even "good" leaders must be regarded with a certain wariness. Leaders are not demigods; they put on their trousers one leg after another just like ordinary mortals. No leader is infallible, and every leader needs to be reminded of this at regular intervals. Irreverence irritates leaders but is their salvation. Unquestioning submission corrupts leaders and demeans followers. Making a cult of a leader is always a mistake. Fortunately hero worship generates its own antidote. "Every hero," said Emerson, "becomes a bore at last."

The signal benefit the great leaders confer is to embolden the rest of us to live according to our own best selves, to be active, insistent, and resolute in affirming our own sense of things. For great leaders attest to the reality of human freedom against the supposed inevitabilities of history. And they attest to the wisdom and power that may lie within the most unlikely of us, which is why Abraham Lincoln remains the supreme example of great leadership. A great leader, said Emerson, exhibits new possibilities to all humanity. "We feed on genius. . . . Great men exist that there may be greater men."

Great leaders, in short, justify themselves by emancipating and empowering their followers. So humanity struggles to master its destiny, remembering with Alexis de Tocqueville: "It is true that around every man a fatal circle is traced beyond which he cannot pass; but within the wide verge of that circle he is powerful and free; as it is with man, so with communities."

1

The Death of a Pharaoh

On October 6, 1981, Egypt's president, Anwar Sadat, sat in a reviewing stand at the parade grounds in Nasar City, a suburb of Cairo. The occasion was the celebration of the eighth anniversary of the 1973 Arab-Israeli War, which was being marked with a huge military parade. Sadat was wearing the brightly decorated uniform of an Egyptian field marshal, his chest adorned with medals and crisscrossed with sashes as he watched the cream of Egypt's armed forces roll past in a fleet of armored personnel carriers. On Sadat's left sat his minister of defense, army lieutenant general Abd al-Halim Abu Ghazala; sitting on Sadat's right was his vice-president, Muhammad Hosni Mubarak.

Oh great people, the best way to commemorate our leader who has fallen in the arena of struggle is that we should unite and continue the struggle so that Egypt will always remain strong and glorious.
—HOSNI MUBARAK
after the death of Sadat

Egyptian president Anwar Sadat (right) and his vice-president, Hosni Mubarak, in 1979. After the assassination of Sadat two years later, Mubarak rose to the presidency, a post he would hold throughout the 1980s and into the 1990s.

U.S. president Jimmy Carter (center) clasps hands with Sadat and Israeli prime minister Menachem Begin at a 1979 White House ceremony marking the signing of the Egyptian-Israeli peace treaty. The treaty, part of a U.S.-brokered agreement called the Camp David peace accords, ended more than 30 years of hostility between Egypt and Israel.

Sadat and the assembled leaders of the Egyptian government watched as truckloads of troops rolled by. In the front seat of one of those trucks sat an army lieutenant named Khaled al-Islambuli, waiting. As his truck neared the reviewing stand, Islambuli pulled out a pistol. He pointed it at the driver and ordered him to stop. The frightened driver slammed on the brakes, causing the truck to swerve out of the parade line. It screeched to a halt near the reviewing stand.

Sadat and those near him did not realize what

was happening. The parade was winding down as planned, and their attention was turned skyward, where Egyptian air force fighter jets roared overhead in tight formation. Amid the din, Lieutenant Islambuli jumped down from the truck. Sadat rose from his seat when he saw Lieutenant Islambuli, perhaps expecting a salute. But what he got instead was an explosion. Islambuli tossed a hand grenade toward the crowd, while three other assassins opened up from the back of the same truck, spraying the reviewing stand with machine-gun fire.

Mubarak later remembered the brief but violent moments of the attack: "I was looking to see the air show, until I heard some noises. . . . Some small explosion happened. I saw President Sadat standing up [and] because whenever he stands we have to stand. The Defense Minister stands, too, to salute the officers. In a second I just saw the image of someone throwing something. Then I was pushed away, and I tried to push President Sadat."

The government security forces and Sadat's bodyguards were caught by surprise, too much in disarray to return fire for as long as 40 seconds. Meanwhile, with two of the assassins providing cover from the left and right flanks of the stand, Islambuli and one of his compatriots ran up to the area near the front row where Sadat had been sitting. Standing on tiptoe, Islambuli pointed his gun at Sadat's prone body, lying under a jumble of chairs that had been piled up as protection by his aides. Islambuli shot several rounds into Sadat. "I am Khaled al-Islambuli," he shouted. "I have killed Pharaoh, and I do not fear death."

Finally the security men began their counterattack. Directing with his baton, Defense Minister Abu Ghazala organized the capture of the assassins, who quickly gave themselves up now that their mission had been accomplished. Eight people, including Sadat, had been killed in the attack. Another 28 were wounded. Among the dead were Sadat's chief aide, General Hassan Allam, and the presidential photographer. The wounded included Mubarak, Abu Ghazala, and three United States military officers who were attached to the U.S. military aid mission.

The U.S. ambassador to Egypt, Alfred L. Atherton, was among those who were sitting in the reviewing stand that day. After the shooting had stopped and the chaos died down, Atherton, who had escaped unharmed, radioed the U.S. embassy in downtown Cairo to inform the State Department in Washington, D.C., about what had happened. But he was unable to determine whether Sadat had been killed. The attack had taken place at about 1:00 P.M. Cairo

God has ordained that Sadat should die on a day that itself is symbolic of him, among his soldiers, heroes and people proudly celebrating the anniversary of the day on which the Arab nation regained its dignity.

—HOSNI MUBARAK
after the death of Sadat

time, and all that afternoon no one was quite sure whether Sadat was still alive. By early evening, however, the government radio and television stations, which had been playing inspirational military music, switched to airing quotations from the Holy Koran.

Later that night, a bandaged and shaken Vice-president Mubarak announced to the world the death of Sadat. "Choked with emotion," Mubarak said, "my tongue is unable to eulogize to the Egyptian nation, the Arab and Islamic people, and the whole world the struggling leader and hero, Anwar Sadat. . . . The leader to whom millions of hearts are attached is martyred." Mubarak's words, however appropriate to the occasion, did not reflect the true feelings of the rest of the Arab world.

The 11 years of Sadat's rule had not been easy for Egypt. Sadat became president upon the death of President Gamal Abdel Nasser, the leader of the 1952 coup that overthrew the Egyptian monarchy, and many Egyptians felt that Sadat was a poor substitute for the charismatic Nasser. Sadat had won some confidence from his people after he guided the Egyptian army to a partial victory in the 1973 war with Israel. And he had won wide praise in North America and Western Europe in the late 1970s, especially after he signed the Camp David peace accords with Israel in 1978. Sadat believed that peace with Israel was Egypt's best chance for economic development and future prosperity, but his people did not agree. Many Egyptians still hated Israel, believing that Israel had unjustly displaced the Palestinians and continued to hold Arab lands, including the holy city of Jerusalem.

Peace with Israel was not the only reason that Sadat was widely disliked by so many of his people. Another reason was his economic policy, called Infitah, an Arabic word meaning "opening." Sadat had started the policy in 1974 to open Egypt to the Western economic powers and investment by foreign corporations. This policy was a radical departure from that of his predecessor, Nasser, who had transformed Egypt's economy into a socialist, state-guided system during the 1950s and 1960s. Nasser's program produced economic stagnancy from the mid-1960s on, and Sadat believed that the nation needed economic reforms to stimulate its moribund economy. But Infitah did not work as Sadat had hoped; while the economy worsened for the vast majority of Egyptians, a handful of the wealthy, including some of the president's friends and advisers, became wealthier still.

Egyptian army lieutenant Khaled al-Islambuli (left) and codefendants stand in a barred holding pen at their trial on charges of killing Sadat. Islambuli and the others, all of them belonging to Islamic fundamentalist groups, admitted to the crime, claiming that they had shot Sadat because he had abandoned Islam for Israel and the United States.

During the 1970s, Sadat's increasingly flamboyant life-style further alienated many Egyptians. He owned many houses throughout the country, wore European clothes and adopted a European manner, and, in the eyes of many critics, acted as though he were an absolute ruler — traits that left many traditional Egyptians cold, particularly in the wake of the 1979 Islamic Revolution that toppled the rule of the shah in Iran. Islamic revival groups, opposed to

A Cairo shop owner laments the damage done by looters in the aftermath of the Sadat assassination. Martial law was imposed to guard against an Islamic fundamentalist coup that never actually materialized.

Sadat's friendship with Israel and the West, developed widespread support in Egypt.

On September 3, 1981, a little more than one month before he was assassinated, Sadat ordered a government crackdown on suspected opponents of his rule. More than 1,500 Egyptians were arrested — including Islamic religious activists, members of Egypt's Coptic Christian minority, intellectuals,

journalists, and even former government officials —
on charges of undermining the government. Several
days after the arrests, Sadat expelled the Soviet
Union's ambassador to Cairo, along with 6 Soviet
diplomats, 2 journalists, and about 1,000 other Soviet citizens working in Egypt. Sadat claimed that
the Soviets had engaged in acts of political subver-
sion. The expulsion of the Soviets was a move that

was greeted warmly in Washington, D.C., although most of the other Arab states, which counted on the Soviet Union for military and economic aid, were shocked.

This was the political landscape that Sadat left behind in the wake of his assassination at the parade grounds. He was mourned in the West and in Israel, but the reaction in the Arab world was different. In Egypt, the response among the general population was muted, in sharp contrast with the deep grief the people had shown upon the death of Nasser, and in some Arab nations, Sadat's death was greeted with jubilation. Almost all of the Arab states had broken off diplomatic relations with Egypt after Sadat had signed the 1978 Camp David peace accords with Israel; the Egyptian president was seen as a traitor for making peace with Israel. In Syria, Iraq, Libya, and the Muslim-dominated western sector of Lebanon's capital, Beirut, people celebrated when they heard of Sadat's death.

On the other hand, in the United States, President Ronald Reagan called Sadat a "champion of peace" and a "close friend" of the United States. Three former U.S. presidents, Richard Nixon, Gerald Ford, and Jimmy Carter, attended Sadat's funeral on October 10, 1981. Israel's prime minister Menachem Begin, with whom Sadat had signed the peace accords, also came, as did dignitaries from more than 80 other nations. Security was tight at the funeral (ordinary Egyptians were not allowed to attend), which took place near the site of the assassination. The president's body was placed in a sarcophagus in the Tomb of the Unknown Soldier — where Sadat himself had placed a memorial wreath not long before he was killed.

Although Sadat's killers were captured by government forces soon after the attack, several outbreaks of antigovernment violence occurred during the days following the assassination. Sadat's killing was to have been part of a wider plot to overthrow the government and set up an Islamic state, based on the model of Ayatollah Khomeini's Islamic Republic of Iran. The most serious of the outbreaks occurred

It is your turn to lead the country now. Please, Mr. Mubarak, take care of Egypt.

—JIHAN SADAT
on hearing the news of her husband's death

in the city of Asyût, a center of Islamic activism about 200 miles south of Cairo. For three days, Egyptian police battled heavily armed Islamic fundamentalists. When the government regained control of Asyût, 50 policemen and a much higher number of the extremists were dead. Some 2,500 people were arrested over the next few days in the government crackdown, and 30 officers and more than 1,000 enlisted men were charged with religious extremism and discharged from the armed forces.

There is still some debate about the role of Egypt's military in the Sadat assassination. The assassins were able to bring loaded machine guns and grenades to a parade where live weapons were prohibited, leading some to believe that the assassination was a military plot. Islambuli was an artillery lieutenant, and the plot's mastermind, Abud al-Zumar, was a former colonel in Egyptian military intelligence. However, no conclusive evidence linking the military establishment to Sadat's assassination was ever made public.

The four men arrested at the parade grounds belonged to an Islamic fundamentalist group called Al-Jihad, or Holy War. During their trial, which began the month after Sadat's killing, the assassins were held in large, barred cages. "I am guilty of killing Sadat and I admit that," Khaled al-Islambuli announced from his cage. "I am proud of it because the cause of religion was at stake."

Meanwhile, the caretaker government had to get on with the business of who would succeed the fallen president. A special election was held on October 13, 1981, to choose Sadat's successor. Mubarak won, which was no surprise; he was the only candidate. He took the oath of office the following day.

From the moment Mubarak took power, it was evident that he would run the country very differently from the way Sadat had run it. Sadat loved cameras and newspaper reporters; Mubarak shunned publicity. Sadat was given to unpredictable actions and policy shifts; Mubarak seemed to

Mubarak speaks to the Egyptian people after being sworn in as president on October 14, 1981.

favor a rational, technocratic way of making decisions.

Mubarak assumed power during a time of national emergency, when rumors of plots to overthrow the government were still in the air. Mubarak, however, felt it was important to reestablish a feeling of normalcy. He ordered the release of some of the political figures Sadat had jailed, among them Egypt's most famous journalist, Muhammad Heikal. Mubarak also released the leader of the largest Islamic group, the Muslim Brotherhood, Umar al-Tilmassani, and the leader of the dissolved opposition New Wafd party, Fuad Serageddin. Striving for unity in a time of national crisis, Mubarak called some of the newly released prisoners to the presidential palace to meet with him.

On November 8, a little more than a month after Sadat's death, Mubarak gave his first major speech as president. Unlike Sadat, who was known to speak for 3 hours at a time, Mubarak gave a concise 45-minute speech in which he said that Egypt would continue to honor its peace treaty with Israel. He also called for a nonaligned policy that favored neither the United States nor the Soviet Union. And Mubarak made Egypt's economic crisis his top priority, pledging "not to commit myself to what I cannot implement, hide the truth from the people, or be lenient with corruption and disorder."

Mubarak's low-key presidency had begun.

2

A New Egypt and a Young Pilot

Muhammad Hosni Mubarak was born on May 4, 1929, in Kafr-el-Meselha in Egypt's Nile delta region, a village where even today chickens and goats run freely on the dirt streets, much as they did when Mubarak was a child.

Mubarak was one of five children; his father was a court officer in Shebin al-Kom, the largest city in the province. Young Mubarak was a good student who often helped his friends with their studies after school. His family connections and good record at school enabled him to gain acceptance to the Egyptian Military Academy in Cairo, and in November 1947 he left home to begin his training there. For Mubarak and many other young Egyptian men of his day, joining the military was the road to political influence and maybe even wealth.

The two main forces in Egyptian politics today are Nasserism and fundamentalism.
—MUHAMMAD HEIKAL
Egyptian political commentator

A view of Cairo, the capital of Egypt, in the 1930s. Mubarak, born in 1929 in a Nile Delta village, came to Cairo in 1947 as a military cadet. Trained as an air force pilot, he rose steadily through the ranks during the next 20 years.

Military power and politics have been tied together throughout Egyptian history. Egypt, situated on the northeastern corner of the African continent, is a crossroads for the cultures of the Middle East and Africa. On the country's southern border is Sudan, on the west is Libya, and on the northeast is Israel. Egypt has two coastlines, the Mediterranean to the north and the Red Sea to the east. The Suez Canal, which cuts through Egyptian territory for its entire length, links the two seas. The Nile River — at more than 4,000 miles the world's longest — flows through Egypt from the Sudanese border in the south to the Mediterranean Sea in the north. The Nile's waters make farming possible in an otherwise arid land.

Egypt's location has made it a center for trade and commerce in the Middle East. The Egyptian people have a strong identity with their land and their ancient civilization. The Arabic name for Egypt is Misr, which means "to civilize" or "to become a populated area." As the historian Afaf al-Sayyid Marsot notes, "Even before the age of nationalism made people conscious of national affinities, Egyptians were conscious of living in a land called Egypt." Indeed, Egypt has been a unified state for more than 5,000 years. The nation's ancient past — especially the age of the pharaohs and the Pyramids, towering statues, and other monumental marvels it left behind — is a source of great pride for the Egyptians.

Egypt has historically been divided into two regions: Upper Egypt and Lower Egypt. These two regions were first united as a single political entity in about 3100 B.C. by a ruler named Menes. The reign of this ruler marks the start of the first of the 30 pharaonic dynasties, which make up ancient Egyptian history. During these long eras, the nation developed high art and culture and a sophisticated political bureaucracy.

Egypt's strategic location between Asia and Africa made it a periodic target of invasion through the ages, and from the Persian conquest in 525 B.C. to the overthrow of the Muhammad Ali dynasty in 1952, the nation was governed by foreigners: Persians, Greeks, Romans, Circassians, Arabs, Turks,

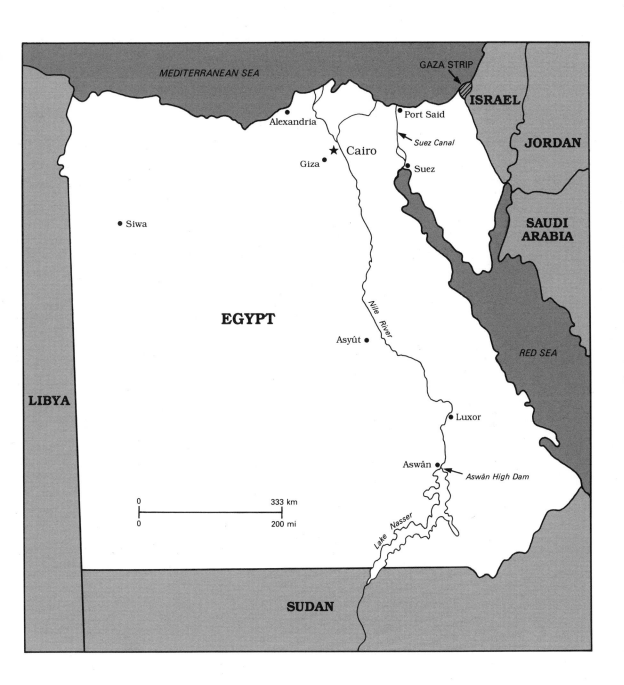

MEDITERRANEAN SEA

GAZA STRIP

ISRAEL

JORDAN

• Port Said

Suez Canal

• Alexandria

★ Cairo

Giza •

• Suez

SAUDI
ARABIA

• Siwa

EGYPT

RED SEA

Nile River

Asyût •

LIBYA

Luxor •

Aswân •

Aswân High Dam

| 0 | | 333 km |
| 0 | | 200 mi |

Lake Nasser

SUDAN

Camel drivers pause before the Great Pyramids and the Sphinx at Giza, in the desert outside Cairo, during the 1920s. Egypt, first united under one ruler around the year 3100 B.C., was home to one of the world's earliest civilizations.

and Britons. Even the army of Napoleon Bonaparte, the French emperor, spent three years in Egypt between 1798 and 1801. Each of these invading powers stamped its own mark on Egyptian society, but only the Arabs were able to transform Egypt on a grand scale.

The religion of Islam emerged in the 7th century A.D. on the Arabian Peninsula, in what is today Saudi Arabia, with the teachings of the prophet Muhammad. In the years following Muhammad's death in A.D. 632, the Arabs' powerful armies swept through half of the Western world in a holy war of

conversion. Palestine, Syria, Iraq, and Persia all fell before the Arab armies, who in turn brought Islam to the peoples they conquered. By 642, the Arabs had defeated an army of the Byzantine Empire and added Egypt to their conquests. The conquerors set up their camp at Al-Fustat, close to what is now Cairo. In addition to Islam, the Arabs brought a new language, Arabic, to Egypt. From then on, Egypt was a part of the Arab world.

Before the Arab conquest, a Christian group called the Copts dominated Egypt, but a great many Copts soon converted to Islam. Today the 3 million to 5 million Copts, who claim to be descendants of the ancient Egyptians, are Egypt's largest religious minority, making up about 10 percent of the total population. At the time of the Arab conquest, the Coptic language was spoken widely throughout the land, but today it is used only in church services.

Within 300 years of the Arab conquest, Arabic was almost the sole language spoken in Egypt, and by the 10th century, Egypt had become the major center for the study of Islamic theology and law. Al-Azhar Mosque, founded in Cairo in 970, became the focus of Islamic learning; it soon evolved into an institution that many consider to be the world's first university.

Part of the Egyptian Military Academy in the late 1940s, when Mubarak was enrolled. The Egyptian military was trained largely by British advisers until 1951.

In 1517, Egypt became part of the Ottoman Empire, a vast but loosely governed Muslim domain whose capital city was Constantinople (now Istanbul) in what is today Turkey. Traditionally, the Ottomans' only interest in their far-flung lands was the collection of taxes. As far as the Ottomans were concerned, the local governors could do whatever they pleased, just as long as the tax revenues were sent to Constantinople on schedule. For almost 300 years Egypt remained a distant but important — and virtually self-governing — outpost of the Ottoman Empire.

In 1798, Napoleon invaded and conquered Egypt. But the French were harassed by the combined mil-

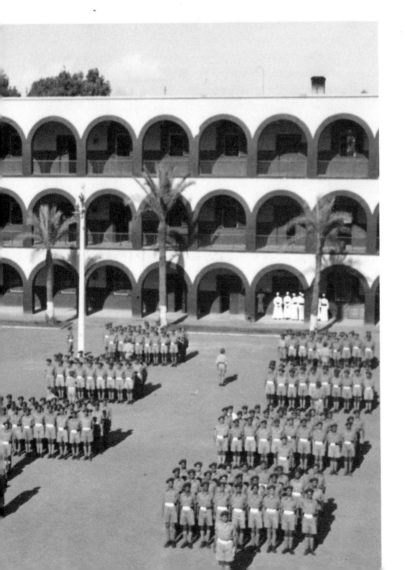

itary forces of Britain and the Ottomans. The French left Egypt in 1801. One of the men fighting them, an officer in the Ottoman army in 1801, was a young man named Muhammad Ali, who would soon become the *pasha*, or governor, of Egypt.

Muhammad Ali Pasha is considered the founder of modern Egypt. He ruled the country in the name of the Ottoman Empire, but he ran it as a virtually independent state. Muhammad Ali brought European technology to Egypt, employing Europeans to set up gun factories, shipyards, paper factories, and textile mills. Cotton production boomed in this period, and today cotton is still the nation's most important export crop.

To defend his new state, Muhammad Ali recruited unemployed French military officers to start a military school at Aswân in Upper Egypt. He also brought Europeans to Egypt to teach modern medicine and engineering. New roads and canals also were built during Muhammad Ali's reign.

In 1839, Muhammad Ali went to war against the Ottoman Empire and won on the battlefield, but the British and French, then allied with the Ottomans, forced him to back down. In 1841, however, the Ottoman ruler appointed Muhammad Ali permanent viceroy of Egypt, with the post to be passed on to his heirs in perpetuity.

Muhammad Ali's descendants did not distinguish themselves as Egypt's rulers. The most notable among them was Ismāʿīl Pasha, who ruled Egypt from 1863 until 1879, when the British and French removed him from power. In the second year of his reign, Egypt became the site of one of the greatest engineering feats of all time when the Suez Canal was completed.

Designed by a Frenchman named Ferdinand-Marie de Lesseps, the canal opened up a new route from the Mediterranean to the Red Sea. Although the canal made Egypt one of the world's economic focal points in the 19th century, Egypt itself had little control over the vast amounts of money that the canal was generating. Britain and France, the Suez Canal's cosponsors, now had a stranglehold on the Egyptian economy.

In 1879, an Egyptian army colonel named Ahmed

Urabi led a nationalist revolt against the British. But British forces crushed the revolt in 1882 and stayed on to occupy Egypt. From 1882 to 1922, Britain ran Egypt as a virtual colony of the British Empire. British citizens living in Egypt during this time did not have to obey Egyptian law; if they committed any crimes or misdemeanors, they were tried in a special court for foreigners. This arrangement was a constant source of humiliation and anger for Egyptian nationalists.

A new generation of Egyptian nationalists emerged in 1918, after the end of World War I. Under the leadership of Sa'd Zaghlūl, the Wafd al-Misri (Egyptian Delegation) called for Egyptian independence. Their efforts finally paid off in 1922, when the British granted the Egyptians partial independence. King Fu'ād, a descendent of Muhammad Ali, was given the throne and granted the responsibility for running Egypt's internal affairs. But the British retained responsibility for the defense of Egypt, the control of foreigners, and control of the Sudan.

Finally, in 1936, the Egyptians and British signed the Anglo-Egyptian Treaty, which ended the British occupation of Egypt. By the terms of the treaty, the British were allowed to keep their troops in the Suez Canal zone until 1956. At the end of World War II, anti-British feelings centered on the continued British rule of the Sudan and the headwaters of the Nile, which Egypt wanted to control so it could manage its fragile agricultural economy. In the late 1940s, Britain announced that it would allow the Sudanese to vote on their own independence, a situation that angered many Egyptian nationalists. But these worries were soon overshadowed by major changes in another British-controlled land in the Middle East: Palestine.

Originally a province of the Ottoman Empire, Palestine became a British-controlled territory after World War I. After World War II ended, thousands of European Jews — most of them survivors of Nazi death camps, where 6 million Jews perished — moved to Palestine. There they joined the population of Jewish settlers who had been working the land for one or two generations as part of an effort to create an independent Jewish state. On Novem-

Bilad micr kheirda li gheirha.
(The land of Egypt, its riches belong to others.)
—Ancient Egyptian proverb

British troops at Cairo's central mosque in 1925. Britain took administrative control of Egypt from the Ottoman Turks in 1882 and in 1914 cut all ties between Egypt and the Ottoman Empire, thus ending 400 years of Turkish rule.

ber 29, 1947, the newly formed United Nations decided to partition Palestine into two independent states: one Arab and one Jewish. But the Palestinian Arabs were not consulted on the issue; they believed that Palestine was entirely theirs.

British rule in Palestine ended on May 15, 1948. On the night of May 14, a Jewish nationalist leader named David Ben-Gurion declared the independence of the State of Israel. The Arab states condemned the new Jewish state. Almost immediately, the military forces of Egypt and four other Arab countries attacked Israel, but the Israelis fought back and won, increasing the amount of territory under Jewish rule in the process. A badly beaten Egypt agreed to sign an armistice with Israel on February 24, 1949.

The loss of the 1948 Palestine War, or War of Independence as it is known in Israel, is central to the next stage of Egyptian history. It was during this war that a young Egyptian army major named Gamal Abdel Nasser first made his mark. Nasser, who had served with distinction and was wounded in action, was disgusted when he learned that the Egyptian high command had been riddled with corruption, leaving the men in the field to fight with old and outdated equipment. Often the soldiers' guns misfired and their grenades sometimes exploded in their hands. Egypt's own King Farouk and many of his friends were said to be siphoning off the money that was allocated to buy new weapons and depositing it in private bank accounts.

In 1949, Nasser and other Egyptian army officers

formed a secret underground group that became known as the Free Officers. After three years of planning, they struck, and on the night of July 22, 1952, the Free Officers overthrew the government. On the morning of July 23, a Free Officer named Anwar Sadat took the microphone at Cairo Radio and informed the Egyptian people that the army had assumed power. Sadat said that Egypt's new leaders would cleanse the nation of corruption, beginning with the king, who was ordered to leave the country.

King Farouk, Egypt's last monarch, was overthrown in 1952 by a group of young Egyptian military officers led by Gamal Abdel Nasser. Sadat belonged to that group. Nasser's government subsequently championed Egyptian and pan-Arab nationalism, instituted socialism, and cut ties with Britain, allying itself instead with the Soviet Union.

On July 26, King Farouk left Egypt for the last time. He sailed to Italy in exile aboard the royal yacht. Soon thereafter, the Revolutionary Command Council, consisting of Nasser and the Free Officers, assumed direct control of the government. On June 18, 1953, Egypt was declared a republic, with General Muhammad Neguib as president.

Nasser soon pushed out Neguib and set the nation on a new path, which he called Arab Socialism. The government took over many private businesses and directed the economy by decree, and a massive social welfare system was installed. On the international scene, Nasser believed in the doctrine of Pan-Arabism, or close economic, political, and cultural alliance between the Arab nations. The political and economic differences between the Arab states, however, often left little room for cooperation.

Hosni Mubarak was a full generation younger than the Free Officers of the 1952 Revolution. He was a 24-year-old air force pilot when Nasser and his associates took over Egypt. After graduating from the Egyptian Military Academy in February 1949, Mubarak had moved on to the Air Academy, from which he graduated in March 1952. As a pilot, he was among the best at flying the British Spitfire fighters.

In the early 1950s, Mubarak went back to the Air Academy to teach other pilots. He was a teacher for seven years. One of Mubarak's student pilots was a brother of Sadat's, who was a member of the Revolutionary Command Council and close to President Nasser.

As a teacher, Mubarak met a new generation of air force men, some of whom would later serve in his presidency. He also met Suzanne Sabet, whose brother was a student pilot under Mubarak's instruction. Mubarak and Sabet were engaged in 1957 and married a year later.

One day Sadat came out to the airfield to watch his brother's performance. It was on this occasion that he and Mubarak first met, and an impressed Sadat jotted down Mubarak's name in his notebook. It was a name he would be hearing more of as time went on.

> *Mustafa Kamel said: "To live in despair is no life." Today we are in the depths of despair.*
> —GAMAL ABDEL NASSER
> former president of Egypt,
> writing in 1937

3

Military Man and Politician

During the early 1950s, many Egyptians were unhappy that the British military was still based in the Suez Canal zone. But in June 1956 the British, as promised in a 1936 treaty, pulled their troops out of the zone. Nevertheless, even after the British soldiers left, the canal itself was still owned by British and French corporations, a situation that many Egyptians resented almost as deeply as the presence of foreign troops. Nasser was as vehement as anyone about the nationalization of the canal.

On July 26, 1956, during a speech celebrating the anniversary of the 1952 Revolution, Nasser suddenly announced: "In the name of the Government of Egypt, I inform you that the Suez Canal Company is nationalized and I have come to take over the premises." The European owners, he said, would have to give up their titles to the canal.

While it is possible to drive the camel at the same time as the automobile, this is no longer possible in the rocket age.
—GAMAL ABDEL NASSER
former president of Egypt

An Egyptian infantryman leaps for cover during the 1956 Suez War, when Israel, Britain, and France invaded Egypt, capturing the Sinai Peninsula and the Suez Canal. It was the second in a string of Egyptian military defeats stretching from the Israeli war of independence in 1948 to the Six-Day War in 1967.

The British and French were furious. For them, the canal was a strategic waterway, an important shortcut for ships traveling from Asia to Europe. Keeping it in British and French hands meant Middle East oil could always make it quickly and efficiently to Europe. Working with the Israelis, they immediately began preparing plans for an invasion.

On October 29, 1956, Israeli troops parachuted into Egypt's Sinai Peninsula. In the coming days a combined British and French force attacked the Egyptian city of Port Said at the northern end of the canal. By November 7, when a cease-fire took effect, the invasion had been a complete military success. The canal had been taken by the British, French, and Israelis.

But international opinion was running against the invaders, and even in Britain the action was unpopular. The Americans, who were opposed to Nasser's nationalization scheme, nevertheless disapproved of the invasion and successfully pressured the British and French to withdraw. By March 1957, the Israeli forces had left the Sinai, too. They were replaced by a United Nations peacekeeping force, and the canal soon reopened under Egyptian control.

So even though Egypt had lost the war on the battlefield, Nasser emerged from the conflict as the proud hero of the Arab world, an inspiration to Arab nationalists who didn't want their countries to be controlled by Europeans anymore. During the period between the Suez War and the 1967 war, Nasser's influence grew. Small nations around the world, opposed to what they saw as American and Western European imperialism, looked to Nasser as their model and spokesman.

But Nasser's chief concern and most fervent dream was the union of the Arab states. In 1958, he engineered the political confederation of Egypt and Syria, which joined together to form the United Arab Republic. But the merger only lasted until September 1961, when Syria withdrew.

Although Nasser relied heavily on the military and financial help of the Soviet Union and its allies, he continued to advocate a policy of nonalignment,

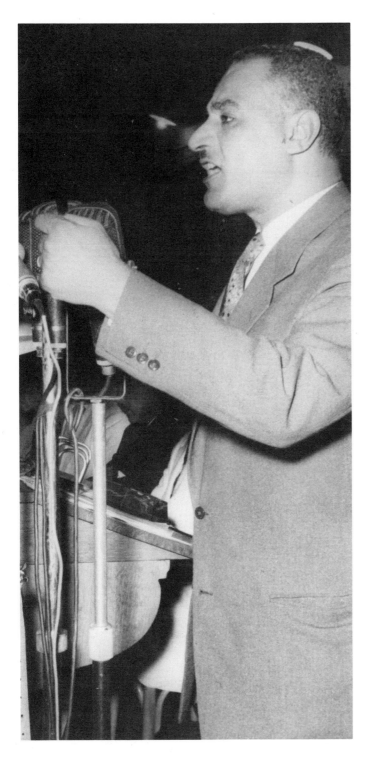

Egyptian president Gamal Abdel Nasser makes his unilateral declaration placing the Suez Canal under the sole jurisdiction of Egypt in July 1956. Britain, France, and Israel responded by invading Egypt.

An Israeli army convoy passes a truck filled with Egyptian soldiers taken prisoner during the Six-Day War in June 1967. Israel captured the West Bank from Jordan, the Golan Heights from Syria, and Sinai and the Gaza Strip from Egypt in its lightning victory.

which at the time meant staying out of alliances with either the Communist East or the capitalist West.

From the mid-1950s to the early 1970s, Egypt was the Soviet Union's major ally in the Middle East. The Soviets supplied Egypt with tanks, planes, arms, and other military equipment, an arrangement that would work to Hosni Mubarak's advantage. Mubarak, the highly regarded teaching pilot, was put in charge of all Soviet-made bomber aircraft in January 1959 and made several trips to the Soviet Union in 1960 and 1961. While there, he trained in Ilyushin-28 and Tupolev-16 bombers.

From February 1964 to April 1965, Mubarak studied at the prestigious Frunze Military Academy in Kirghizia in Soviet Central Asia, where he learned to speak Russian. But despite this experience Mubarak is said to dislike the Soviets; today he is known as an anti-Communist who disapproved of Egypt's former reliance on the Soviet Union for military equipment.

In 1962, Mubarak was sent to Yemen for a short time to take command of Egyptian bomber aircraft during the civil war there. The Egyptians intervened on the side of the Communist rebels who had overthrown the local monarchy. Egypt's participation in the conflict in Yemen lasted from 1962 to 1967. At the height of Egypt's involvement, there were almost 75,000 Egyptian soldiers in Yemen, a substantial drain on Egypt's economy. And Nasser's support for the Communists put Egypt in conflict with the Saudi Arabian government, which backed the royalists.

The worsening Arab-Israeli crisis of the mid-1960s diverted Nasser's attention from Yemen. Egypt and Syria sent troops to their borders with Israel in the spring of 1967, but the first blow was struck by the Israelis. In a lightning attack on June 5, Israeli air force fighter-bombers destroyed the Egyptian, Jordanian, Syrian, and Iraqi air forces. A United Nations cease-fire went into effect on June 11, but in those six days of warfare, the Israelis conquered huge chunks of Egyptian, Jordanian, and Syrian territory. Israel took the Gaza Strip on the Mediterranean coast and the entire Sinai Peninsula from Egypt; East Jerusalem and the land on the West Bank of the Jordan River from Jordan; and the Golan Heights from Syria — one of the quickest, most astonishing military victories ever won. Except for the Sinai Peninsula, which was returned to Egypt under the terms of the 1979 Egypt-Israel peace treaty, Israel still occupies the lands it captured in the Six-Day War of 1967.

What was for the Israelis a glorious victory was for the Arabs a humiliating defeat. The Egyptians were especially humiliated, for once again their forces had been resoundingly crushed by the Israelis. Government investigations were launched to assign blame for the disaster. Nasser himself offered to resign, but the offer was declined.

The defeat was blamed on the military, and Nasser fired many officers. This was a very important step for Egypt, and for Mubarak, because it cleared the way for younger officers to move up in rank.

In November 1967, Mubarak was chosen to be director general of the Egyptian Air Academy. He acquitted himself well in the post, and in June 1969 Nasser appointed Mubarak chief of staff of the air force. The job of the 41-year-old Mubarak was to rebuild the Egyptian air force into an efficient fight-

ing machine capable of taking on — and beating —
the Israelis.

Both Sadat and Mubarak had come a long way
from the day they first met in the early 1950s. On
December 20, 1969, Nasser appointed Sadat to be
Egypt's vice-president. On September 28 of the fol-
lowing year, Nasser died. Seventeen days later,
Sadat became Egypt's president.

An Arab in New York City
mourns Nasser's death in
1970. An enormously popu-
lar figure in the Arab world,
Nasser was replaced by
Sadat, who eventually
earned the hostility of most
Arabs by courting the West
and making peace with
Israel.

During the early 1970s, Sadat started to stamp his imprint on Egypt. First, he began to distance his government from the Soviet Union, whose arms sales to Egypt rarely included sophisticated weaponry. When the Soviet government did send advanced weapons systems to Egypt, they also sent Soviet army personnel to run the equipment and barred Egyptian technicians from the sites. To Sadat and many other Egyptians, this policy smacked of the foreign domination and special privileges for Europeans that was supposed to have been abolished decades before.

In July 1972, Sadat expelled the Soviets. A high-ranking Egyptian air force general protested the move, and Sadat promptly fired him, choosing Mubarak as his replacement. Now Mubarak had two jobs: commander in chief of the air force and deputy minister of war.

With Mubarak in control of the air force, Sadat initiated plans for a strike against the Israeli forces occupying the Sinai. Throughout 1973, the Egyptians secretly trained for a lightning move across the Suez Canal, a thrust into the Sinai, and then a doubling-back maneuver that would encircle and trap the Israeli forces on the east bank of the waterway. The date chosen for the attack was October 6, the most solemn day of the Jewish calendar, Yom Kippur.

The majority of the Israeli officers and soldiers were fasting and worshiping when the Egyptians launched their attack, which was coordinated to coincide with a Syrian assault against the Israeli-held Golan Heights far to the northeast. After 24 hours of fierce fighting, Egyptian forces succeeded in crossing the canal and breaking through the massive Israeli fortifications known as the Bar Lev Line on the east bank of the waterway.

Under Mubarak's direction, the Egyptian air force performed well, carrying out effective air strikes against Israeli targets in the Sinai. Even so, losses were heavy; Sadat would later claim that Egypt lost 120 airplanes, although the actual number was closer to 200.

After several days the Israelis began to recover the initiative. Even while some of their units were encircled and holding off the Egyptians on the canal's east bank, some Israeli forces managed to cross over to the west bank, trapping the Egyptian Third Army. A deadlock developed. When the United Nations offered a cease-fire, both sides accepted. It was put into effect on October 24, 1973, and the armies returned to their pre-October positions.

The war was not a military success for Egypt. But it wasn't a total failure, either. The Egyptian people were happy to learn that their army had managed the psychological victory of crossing the Suez Canal and engaging the Israelis on the other side. The generation of Egyptian military officers who had taken part in the 1973 war became known as the October Generation. Mubarak was hailed as a hero, and on February 19, 1974, Sadat made him the air marshal of the Egyptian air force.

After the war, Egyptian and Israeli officers met to discuss the cease-fire and a possible exchange of prisoners. These talks later turned into broader discussions about possible peace. The U.S. secretary of state, Henry Kissinger, got involved in these talks and traveled back and forth between Cairo and Jerusalem so often that the newspapers began to refer to the trips as "shuttle diplomacy."

Soon Kissinger helped hammer out an agreement for the disengagement of forces along the Suez Canal, which was signed on January 17, 1974. According to the agreement, the Israeli forces would leave the east bank of the canal but could stay farther inland in the Sinai. A United Nations peacekeeping force would be stationed on the small strip of land running down the length of the canal's east bank, separating the Israeli and Egyptian armies.

In April 1975, Sadat fired his vice-president, Hussein Shafei, one of the last members of Nasser's original Revolutionary Command Council still in the government, and replaced him with his own man — Hosni Mubarak.

The vice-presidency was Mubarak's first nonmilitary job, and his political views were virtually un-

> *Many in Egypt saw Sadat's failure as at least partly the result of the government's close relationship with the United States.*
> —MARK TESSLER
> Middle East historian

Vice-president Mubarak with Israeli prime minister Begin in Cairo in April 1979. It was the first time an Israeli leader made an official visit to an Arab country, and it marked the normalization of relations between Egypt and the Jewish state.

known. His low-key style contributed to a growing belief that he was a political lightweight whose primary function was to rubber-stamp everything Sadat said and did. Before long, people began to call Mubarak La Vache Qui Rit, or the Laughing Cow. This was the name of a bland French cheese spread sold in Cairo groceries. The Laughing Cow label continues to be heard among Mubarak's critics even today.

But in reality Vice-president Mubarak played a more active role than many of his critics believed. In public, Mubarak was quiet and reserved. He quietly sat in on many of Sadat's meetings. He would laugh discreetly at the president's jokes. But behind the scenes, Mubarak began to take a more active role in Egypt's foreign policy, often meeting with regional and national leaders during trips abroad with Sadat. In 1976, Mubarak tried negotiating an end to the guerrilla war in the Western Sahara between Morocco and the rebels fighting for independence. Also in 1976, Mubarak headed an official Egyptian delegation to the People's Republic of China. And in 1980, Mubarak made two trips to the United States.

Mubarak supported Sadat's search for peace and took part in the Camp David negotiations. Sadat was known to have favored some sort of treaty with Israel since the early 1970s. He believed that Egypt had contributed the most and suffered the most in the Arab world's confrontations with Israel; after a quarter century of conflict, the enormous military expenditures needed to finance the armed forces had helped ruin the Egyptian economy. Sadat believed that peace with Israel — and a better relationship with the United States, the world's richest nation — offered the best chance of economic prosperity.

In a November 9, 1977, speech to the Egyptian People's Assembly, President Sadat declared:

> I state in all seriousness that I am prepared to go to the end of the world — and Israel will be surprised to hear me tell you that I am ready to go to their home, to the Knesset [the Israeli parliament] itself, to argue with them, in order to prevent one Egyptian soldier from being wounded. . . . We have no time to waste.

Sadat reckoned that if there was to be peace in the region, the United States would have to be involved. The Americans, after all, were Israel's strongest ally, and U.S. aid was perhaps the main thing keeping Israel's economy afloat. At the same time, several American oil companies, which had very close ties to the U.S. government, owned highly profitable wells and refineries in Arab countries. The Americans, Sadat figured, wanted peace in the Middle East to keep the flow of Arab oil to the United States unimpeded.

Later that November, Sadat made a historic trip to Jerusalem to give a speech before the Knesset. It was a bold, almost unthinkable step, one that impressed the Americans as much as the Israelis. The door to a permanent peace treaty between Egypt and Israel was now open.

In September 1978, Sadat, Israeli prime minister Menachem Begin, and U.S. president Jimmy Carter went into seclusion at the presidential retreat in Camp David, Maryland, to hammer out a peace settlement. Two weeks later they emerged, and on September 17, at an outdoor ceremony at the White House, the three leaders signed the Camp David

Members of an Israeli tank crew wave as they withdraw from Egyptian territory in February 1974 as part of the UN-sponsored cease-fire arrangement that ended the 1973 October War. The October War, in which Israel and Egypt fought to a draw, marked the first time that the Egyptian military held its own against the Israelis.

peace accords, which Sadat and Carter called a "cornerstone" for a comprehensive peace settlement in the Middle East.

The Camp David accords stipulated that Israel would return the Sinai to Egypt and that Egypt and Israel would open diplomatic relations and commercial exchanges. The accords also provided for a possible settlement regarding the issue of Palestinian autonomy in the Israeli-occupied territories of the West Bank and Gaza, two regions captured by Israel in the 1967 war. The formal Egyptian-Israeli peace treaty was signed on March 26, 1979, in Washington, D.C.

The Arab world reacted negatively to the negotiations and to the peace treaty. Sadat had already broken diplomatic relations with the Arab countries of Algeria, Libya, Syria, Iraq, and Yemen after they roundly criticized his 1977 trip to Jerusalem. After

the Camp David accords were signed, all of the Arab states, except for Oman, Sudan, and Somalia, broke off relations with Cairo. Egypt was expelled from Pan-Arabist groups such as the Arab League and the Islamic Conference Organization. The Arab League moved its headquarters from Cairo to Tunis, the capital of Tunisia, as a result of the expulsion. The peace treaty also brought thousands of angry student protesters out into the streets of Cairo.

But for all the rancor that Sadat's actions caused in the Arab world, in Western Europe and North America he was hailed as a heroic man of peace. In 1978, Sadat and Begin were awarded the Nobel Peace Prize, the West's highest honor for world leaders. Still, as the 1970s drew to a close, the big question remained: Could Sadat, the man who made peace with Egypt's mortal enemy, win back the trust of his people?

4

President Mubarak

The assassination of Sadat and the subsequent absence of grief exhibited by most Egyptians were ample evidence of his failure to win the hearts of his people. The lesson did not go unheeded by Mubarak, who made it clear right from the start that the style of his presidency would be a radical departure from that of his flamboyant predecessor. By stressing highly moral values in his first speech as president, Mubarak seemed to distance himself from the grand promises that marked Sadat's oratory.

And indeed, Mubarak would prove to be quite a different kind of president than Nasser and Sadat. While Nasser loved political debate and Sadat loved the international social whirl, Mubarak remains a very private person who sometimes seems uncomfortable in large groups or formal social settings. He is an introvert, a technician more than a politician,

I never tell lies or slogans to our people. I tell them facts and figures. I say only things I am sure of.
—HOSNI MUBARAK

Mubarak faces reporters during a visit to the United States. In contrast to Sadat's highly flamboyant public persona, Mubarak chose a more self-effacing style of governing that stressed efficiency. While not wishing to alienate the Israelis and Americans, he strove to reforge Egypt's links to the Arab world.

Sadat's half brother Esmat defends himself during his trial on corruption charges in 1983. One of Mubarak's first acts as president was to launch government investigations of businessmen accused of illegal practices during the Sadat presidency.

who aims for precision — an approach befitting a man trained as a bomber pilot. When Mubarak was still an active pilot, a military intelligence report described him as "totally businesslike" with "no political tendencies or loyalties."

Mubarak, who as vice-president once said that "everything should be done quietly and not in a dramatic way," set a structured daily regimen for himself that contrasted sharply with Sadat's regal routine. Sadat would rise late in the morning and

conduct much of the day's official business while
sitting in the garden next to his house; Mubarak,
on the other hand, would get up early and set to
work at his office in Cairo's Ouruba Palace. Sadat
quit early and would often go on extended walks in
the countryside; Mubarak's only break during the
day would be time off for a game of squash.

When Sadat was president, his wife, Jihan, and
other family members were celebrities who constantly turned up not only in the Egyptian media

but also in the international media. Jihan Sadat also had a large office staff working for her. So ostentatious was the Sadat family that many Egyptians believed they were siphoning off money from the national treasury. After his death, special attention was focused on Sadat's half brother Esmat, a bus driver who became a millionaire with holdings estimated at $150 million. In February 1983, an Egyptian ethics court found Esmat Sadat and three of his sons guilty of profiteering, sentencing them to one year in jail and confiscating a substantial amount of money and property. Seven other members of the Sadat family were also found guilty in the case.

> *Whenever there is a change in the main structure, we discuss it with many people. Psychologically, the people are more relaxed than before.*
> —HOSNI MUBARAK

The Esmat Sadat case was one of many prosecuted under Mubarak, who directed the Egyptian police and courts to crack down on those found guilty of illegal acquisition of land, black marketeering, and other illicit activities. Mubarak wanted to send a message to those who had become rich through the corruption that thrived under Sadat.

Mubarak also sent a message to the lively Egyptian press, directing them not to publish photos of his wife, Suzanne, or their children. This is one of the reasons that Suzanne, the daughter of an Egyptian doctor and an English nurse, has never achieved the international celebrity for which Jihan Sadat is noted.

But Suzanne Mubarak's life has its fascinating features. During the early years of their marriage, Mubarak was away from home for much of the time. She recalls "the feeling of seeing him packing up in the middle of the night to go on a mission" as the most vivid memory of being the wife of a military man. "You have to live with it and just try to push it away from your mind, but it is there. . . . It was a very hard life." After raising their two sons, Gamal and Alaa, Mrs. Mubarak decided to attend the American University in Cairo, where she completed a combined graduate degree in sociology and anthropology in 1982. Yet few of her professors or fellow students knew that she was the president's wife because she used her maiden name, Sabet, during her entire tenure at the university.

Suzanne Mubarak has accompanied her husband on many of the trips he takes abroad, but as her university experience illustrates, she prefers an extremely low public profile. After Mubarak became president in 1981, a Cairo journalist telephoned to ask for an interview with the first lady of Egypt. He was told that there was no such person.

After Mubarak became president, many of Sadat's advisers were accused of financial wrongdoing. Sadat had built a large informal group of advisers with many ties to the wealthy class that grew up in the era of economic opening. In contrast, Mubarak hired newcomers for jobs in his administration.

Two of Sadat's top advisers, Osman Ahmed Osman and Sayed Marei, were among the richest men in Egypt. Both men had sons who married Sadat's daughters. After Mubarak became president, Osman and Marei were told that their services would not be needed in the new administration. As president, Mubarak relied on advice from Osama el-Baz. Baz, a specialist in foreign affairs, studied at Harvard University in Massachusetts. As chief of staff, Baz has written many of Mubarak's speeches.

Even though Mubarak had been Sadat's vice-president, many Egyptians did not associate Mubarak with Sadat's economic policies or with Camp David. As the 1980s progressed, many Egyptians became increasingly unhappy with both these Sadat initiatives.

In his acceptance speech for the Egyptian presidential nomination, on October 7, 1981, Mubarak said: "I pledge to God and the great Egyptian people to be loyal to the fulfillment of their aspiration and to complete the procession along the road of freedom, democracy, prosperity and peace." But the road has not always been so smooth. Some Egyptians believe Mubarak's government possesses a large security apparatus to keep a lid on dissent. Moreover, the Mubarak government has not rescinded the state of emergency law put into effect after Sadat's assassination. This law has allowed the government to arrest and hold large groups of

> *Mubarak has convinced the opposition groups that they have an interest in keeping him in power, if only to preserve the freedom of expression that they now enjoy.*
> —STANLEY REED
> journalist, *The Nation*

people. The government believes the law is necessary to keep the peace. Nevertheless, Egyptians have had more political freedom and more freedom of the press recently than they have had at any time since the 1952 Revolution.

Mubarak likes to give the impression that he is listening to the voice of the Egyptian people. If he is really listening, his people are sending him different messages — some good and some not so good. There are six legally recognized political parties in Egypt. Mubarak's party is called the National Democratic party (NDP). Mubarak became secretary-general of the NDP in April 1975. The other five parties make up the opposition.

It was Mubarak, in fact, who allowed Egypt's opposition parties to reemerge. Nasser saw political parties as remnants of the corrupt past. In 1953, he outlawed them. In 1977, however, Sadat allowed the parties to form again. But the new political freedom frightened Sadat, and in 1980 he clamped down on all opposition groups. He did not allow the major opposition parties to run candidates in the 1980 election. A constitutional amendment was passed on May 23, 1980, to make Sadat the president for life. At the time of Sadat's death there was only one party, Sadat's NDP. But the political situation would be very different under Mubarak.

In Egypt today, the five legal opposition parties are the Wafd party, the Socialist Labor party, the Progressive Unionist party, the Liberal party, and the Umma party. The Wafd, the Liberal, and the Umma parties are considered to be in the center or on the conservative right. The Socialist Labor and Progressive Unionist parties are considered to be left of center. The conservative parties want more private business. They want to break up the massive state bureaucracy and social welfare system that Nasser set up in the 1960s. The more leftist-oriented parties are hoping for a more equal distribution of wealth. They support state welfare subsidies. While the opposition parties differ in ideology, they also have some of the same goals. They all favor the policy of nonalignment between the United States and the

Soviet Union. They want a more pro-Arab foreign policy. And they want to move away from the relationship with Israel.

Two groups pose a challenge to Mubarak. One is a small but powerful class of businessmen called the Mungatihun, who profited during the Sadat years and were often the target of government investigation in the early Mubarak years.

The other group is the sometimes violent Muslim Brotherhood, an Islamic fundamentalist movement. Although it is not legally constituted as a political party, the Muslim Brotherhood has shown itself to be a significant political force. Under Mubarak, the Brotherhood has become very popular. It has joined with other opposition parties to run candidates in Egyptian elections. In the 1984 and 1987 elections, Brotherhood candidates won seats in the Egyptian parliament. The Brotherhood wants to break the nation's ties with Israel and wants to institute Islamic religious law (called Sharia law) in Egypt. A number of more secretive Islamic groups also challenge Mubarak's presidency.

On May 27, 1984, Egyptian voters went to the polls to vote for 448 parliamentary representatives. For the first time ever, all 5 opposition parties were allotted 40 minutes each on state-run radio and television stations to outline their platforms in public. The government also let the parties hold election rallies in support of their candidates.

For the 1984 election, the Muslim Brotherhood joined the Wafd party, and the combined ticket managed to pull in 12.7 percent of the vote. Mubarak's NDP, however, received an overwhelming 87.3 percent and won 391 of the 448 seats.

Mubarak called the 1984 election a turning point for Egyptian democracy. But the opposition parties complained of corruption. They charged that voting irregularities had taken place. They also claimed that NDP supporters had stuffed ballot boxes in favor of their candidates. In truth, there seemed to be less cheating than in past elections. But Egyptians had already lost faith in Egyptian politics and many chose to stay home on election day.

Mubarak, his son Muhammad Gamal, and his wife, Suzanne, meet with an Ontario government official in 1983. While Sadat's family was constantly in the spotlight during the 1970s, Mubarak's family took a low-profile approach in the 1980s.

On April 6, 1987, Egyptian voters again went to the polls. As in 1984, the turnout was low. Mubarak's critics charged that the ruling NDP had inflated the election returns in their favor. There were 14.3 million people eligible to vote. According to official counts, 7.7 million people voted. But many believe that the real number was probably much smaller.

Compared to 1984, Mubarak's NDP did not do as

well in the 1987 parliamentary elections, winning 308 of the 448 seats. This time the Muslim Brotherhood joined with the Socialist Labor and Liberal parties and made a much stronger showing but was still dwarfed by the NDP's enormous majority. A free electoral process was slowly making gains in Egypt, but the NDP's campaign goals — "stability, development, and democracy"—were still a long way off.

5

Mubarak's Challenges

Once Mubarak had settled into the presidency, Egyptian political life took on a relatively placid rhythm, but as the 1980s wore on, it became clear that he would face a stiff challenge from the Islamic fundamentalist movement then sweeping the Muslim world. A group of fundamentalists had already assassinated Sadat, and after an initial wait-and-see period with Mubarak, they renewed their calls for the imposition of a new Egyptian constitution based on the Koran.

Months of foment finally came to a head when fundamentalists clashed with the government in late February 1986. It was to be the most severe episode of domestic unrest since the Islamic fundamentalist uprising that followed Sadat's assassination.

On the evening of February 25, 1986, Egyptian army troops went on a rampage. They burned and sacked expensive hotels and nightclubs near the Pyramids just outside Cairo. As the hotels burned,

They eat meat, we get bread.
—Rioters chanting outside an expensive tourist hotel in Cairo

Mubarak and his top military officials visit Egypt's Tomb of the Unknown Soldier as part of ceremonies marking Israel's 1982 withdrawal from the Sinai Peninsula. Mubarak was key to his country's relative success in the 1973 war against Israel that helped set in motion the Camp David peace process.

Islamic fundamentalists hold the Koran aloft as they demonstrate against the Mubarak government in 1982. Ired by Sadat and Mubarak's courting of the West and fueled by radical Islamic movements throughout the Muslim world, Islamic fundamentalists clashed frequently with the government in the 1980s.

horrified tourists ran for their lives. The riot had started when soldiers of the Central Security Forces (CSF) heard rumors that they would have to stay in the military for four years instead of three. The CSF, the worst treated and lowest paid of all Egypt's armed forces, is composed primarily of young men recruited from peasant villages; their main job is guarding foreign embassies and major government buildings in the cities. At the time of the riot, each recruit received a monthly salary of just six Egyptian pounds per month, then the equivalent of about four U.S. dollars.

According to newspaper reports, 17,000 of the CSF's 300,000-member force participated in the riot, which threatened to turn into a full-scale mutiny. When the rampaging CSF troops entered Cairo itself, young Islamic fundamentalists joined in. Nightclubs along the road leading to the Pyramids were especially hard hit; those that sold alcohol, which is forbidden under strict Islamic law, were set ablaze by Islamic groups chanting "Allah-o-akhbar" ("God is great").

As the rioting continued, shootings and attacks spread to the city's wealthy enclaves. In the suburb of Maadi, home of many Americans and other foreigners attached to embassies or corporations, CSF troops assigned to guard the neighborhood fired on their officers. Soon Cairo was in chaos, and the revolt spread to the cities of Ismailia and Asyût.

In an effort to regain order, the Mubarak government imposed a curfew in all major cities. The broad boulevards and narrow side streets of Cairo were deserted except for groups of heavily armed soldiers on patrol. Heavy gunfire rang out in some of the wealthier neighborhoods where CSF mutineers held out against forces loyal to Mubarak. By day, government helicopters flew low overhead; at night, glowing red tracer bullets cut across the sky in poor

A burned-out bus in the Cairo suburb of Helwan stands as mute testimony to the March 1986 security forces riots in which anti-Mubarak protests by low-paid government troops and Islamic fundamentalists turned into a destructive rampage.

neighborhoods and other fundamentalist strong-
holds. Military checkpoints were set up on major
roads and armored cars guarded key government
buildings.

It took Egypt's regular armed forces three days to
put down the revolt, which had been fomented, according to Mubarak, by "a deviationist minority."
The official death toll climbed to 107, with more
than 3,700 people arrested and taken into custody.

One aspect of the uprising that surprised many
observers was the accuracy of the news and infor-
mation that the Mubarak regime broadcast to
Egypt's citizens. This new openness was a departure from the way the Mubarak government treated

an earlier crisis, in November 1985, when Egyptian forces tried to rescue an Egypt Air airliner that had been hijacked to Malta. During the incident, Egyptian government radio announced that the plane had been stormed by Egyptian commando forces. It failed to mention, however, that 57 passengers had been killed in the operation. Egyptians had to listen to short-wave broadcasts of the British Broadcasting Corporation to find out what had really happened in Malta.

Violent social unrest is not a new phenomenon in Egypt, and it is often bound up with struggles within Muslim society. Islam is divided into two major groups, the Sunnis and the Shiites, and in Egypt more than 80 percent of the population is Sunni Muslim. Hosni Mubarak is himself a Sunni Muslim. "I am a religious man, but not an extremist." Mubarak has said. "I am a very moderate religious man."

After the 1967 defeat by Israel, Egyptians in growing numbers rejected secular society and the imposition of Western culture and turned increasingly to religion. After the signing of the Camp David accords and the subsequent influx of U.S. aid, the feeling persisted among many Egyptians that their country's relationship with the United States was just as exploitative as it had been with the Soviet Union. In 1986 some graffiti written on the wall of an Islamic school in Upper Egypt read We Need Islam — No East, No West. Next to the message were drawings of an American flag and a Soviet flag, both with lines drawn through them.

The most prominent fundamentalist group during the first 10 years of Mubarak's presidency was the Muslim Brotherhood, which operated within the political system. Many other groups also challenged the state, some of them resorting to violence. But the Islamic groups held some basic principles in common: They categorically rejected the peace treaty with Israel and strenuously objected to Egypt's alliance with the United States. Most important, they all wanted to establish Sharia, or Koranic, law in Egypt as the cornerstone for a national return to what they believed were traditional Islamic values.

Not far from the glittering casinos and $3,000-a-month apartments, millions of Egyptians eke out survival in decaying buildings along narrow, winding alleys surfaced with dirt and slime.
—JOHN BARNES
journalist, *U.S. News and World Report*

A Muslim couple in traditional dress stroll along a Cairo street in 1988. The Islamic fundamentalism that swept the Muslim world in the aftermath of the 1979 Iranian Revolution found a foothold in the Egypt of Sadat and Mubarak.

The Sharia is a body of law based on the Holy Koran and other Islamic texts. The Sharia touches upon almost every area of human activity, from personal cleanliness to taxes to sexual activity. Although the 1980 Egyptian constitution says that the Sharia shall be the "principal" source of law in Egypt, in actuality Egyptian law is much more deeply influenced by Ottoman, Napoleonic, and British common law.

The Islamic groups were not active during the first two years of the Mubarak presidency. When he took power, Mubarak tried to placate Islamic activists by attempting to reestablish ties with other Arab states and by turning down Israel's invitations to visit Jerusalem. Mubarak's handling of the men who killed Sadat also signaled his desire not to antagonize the fundamentalists. The assassins' trial ended in March 1982, and although Islambuli, the other three killers, and several others involved in the plot were sentenced to death, the sentences for some of the other defendants were considered light. Clearly, Mubarak was trying to make peace with the Muslim Brotherhood and the more radical Islamic activists.

But all that changed in 1984, when the Muslim Brotherhood participated in Egypt's parliamentary elections for the first time in 40 years. At the start of the Mubarak era, the Brotherhood was a relatively moderate organization, but it had had a violent past and had been outlawed by both Nasser and Sadat. The Muslim Brotherhood, or Al-Ikhwan Al-Muslimun, as it is known in Arabic, was founded in 1928 by an Egyptian named Hassan al-Banna. In the 1940s, the Brotherhood carried out a series of bombings and assassinations of government officials in Cairo. In 1949, al-Banna himself was killed, allegedly by government agents. After the assassination, the Brotherhood went underground.

In 1954, a Brother tried to kill Nasser at a rally in the Egyptian coastal city of Alexandria. Police rounded up many Brothers, executing several. In 1965, Nasser claimed that the Brotherhood was again trying to kill him. Another government crackdown followed, and yet another Brotherhood leader,

Sayyid Qutb, was put to death. In the 1970s, Sadat reversed Nasser's policy and encouraged the formation of Islamic groups, but by the end of the decade the Brotherhood became one of Sadat's most powerful opponents. The party did well in the 1984 parliamentary elections, a signal of the widespread support that Islamic fundamentalists enjoyed among the Egyptian people.

During the 1970s, several smaller radical Islamic groups formed. The smaller groups, called *gama'at*, are made up of young men who challenge the rule of the state, which they see as corrupt. The number of gama'ats has been estimated at anywhere from 35 to 200 throughout Egypt. Members of one of these groups, Al-Jihad, killed Sadat. Islamic student societies also became popular during the Nasser and early Sadat periods, when young Arab political nationalists filled the campuses. Male students, wearing a full beard and the traditional flowing gown, the *gallibiya*, and female students, wearing the traditional *hijab* head covering, moderated their stance somewhat under Mubarak but remained a potent force in Egyptian politics.

In 1985, there was a showdown between the government and the Islamic activists. In mid-June, an Islamic group headed by Sheikh Hafez Salama marched through the streets of Cairo to support Sharia law. The government responded by arresting Salama and scores of his supporters.

Mubarak has had problems — some of them inherited from Sadat's regime — in Egypt's Coptic community as well. In Cairo in mid-1981, fighting broke out between Copts and Muslims, and Sadat ordered the arrest of the Coptic leader, Pope Shenuda. The pope was confined to the desert monastery of Wadi Natroun. Mubarak kept Shenuda under house arrest for more than three years, which angered the Coptic community. Finally, on the night of January 6, 1985, Coptic Christmas Eve, Mubarak released him.

During the summer of 1985, Copts and Muslims engaged in what became known as the Bumper Sticker War. Automobile drivers in Cairo began put-

Pope Shenuda, leader of Egypt's Coptic church, in 1985, after Mubarak ordered his release from a desert monastery where he had been confined under house arrest for four years. The Coptic Christians — about 10 percent of Egypt's 55 million people — have long clashed with the nation's Sunni Muslim majority.

ting religious stickers on their cars. The most popular Islamic sticker read There Is No God but Allah, and Muhammad Is His Prophet, the Muslim creed. The Copts replied with their own stickers featuring crosses, pictures of Pope Shenuda, and a message reading The Lord Is My Shepherd. Tensions between the two groups became so intense that the government threatened to fine people and take away their driver's license if they continued putting religious stickers on their cars.

Strapped for money, the Egyptian government has been unable to provide adequate services for many of its citizens. In the late 1980s, Islamic groups proved they could sometimes provide better services than the government, setting up schools, small hospitals, clinics, banks, and investment and insurance companies.

The strength of the Islamic groups' challenge to Mubarak is largely the result of Egypt's economic difficulties, which are in turn intensified by the country's population explosion. Approximately 3 million people lived in Egypt during the time of Napoleon's occupation in 1798–1801; the population in 1990 stood at more than 55 million. Every 10 months, 1 million Egyptians are born — a new baby every 21 seconds.

The flash point of the population explosion is Cairo, which has grown enormously, even grotesquely, since the end of World War II. From 1947 to 1966, the Egyptian capital's population doubled from 2 million to 4 million people, and in 1987 about 14 million Egyptians resided in the city and its suburbs. Most of the influx was made up of poor people moving from the countryside in a futile search for jobs.

The rapidly expanding population has left Egypt and especially Cairo with an acute housing shortage. In Cairo in the 1980s, people were forced to live among the tombs and mausoleums in the City of the Dead, Cairo's famous cemetery. Elsewhere in the capital, large families often live in two-room apartments, with three family members crowded into the same bed. Young Cairene couples often put off marriage for years until they can find a home.

And even when they find an apartment, it may be unsafe to live in. Many of the buildings in Cairo are structurally unsound; an estimated 2,000 to 3,000 buildings collapse each year.

The juxtaposition of appalling overcrowding and poverty with wealth is a constant in Cairo, as in most of the world's big cities. The Mercedes-Benz sedans of rich Egyptians cross paths with the donkey-drawn carts of the poor in the streets of the capital. During Sadat's Infitah of the 1970s, skyscrapers sprouted in the city's business districts and expensive consumer goods appeared in shop windows. But amid the newfound wealth, the poor remained poor. Even though workers' salaries went up in the 1970s, pay raises were eaten up by an even higher rise in the cost of living. The situation worsened under Mubarak in the 1980s.

The government has attempted to cope with these problems by building new factories. At the end of the 1980s, Mubarak initiated construction of a model industrial city, called the Tenth of Ramadan, which rises out of the desert about 35 miles outside Cairo. By the year 2000, Egyptian planners hope to have 500,000 people living in the Tenth of Ramadan. The enormous project puts another strain, however, on the resources provided by the Nile River, the nation's lifeblood. The Nile Valley, home to 99 percent of Egypt's population, is a thin strip of green fertile land surrounded by desert on both sides. Yet planners wonder how much longer the Nile can sustain the growing number of Egyptians.

By 1990, Egypt's foreign debt had risen to $46 billion, which was owed to the United States, the Soviet Union, other Arab nations, and the nations of Western Europe. Mubarak turned to the International Monetary Fund (IMF) and the World Bank, two enormous international procapitalist loan organizations, for help during the debt crisis. The United States is the major contributor to both the IMF and the World Bank.

The IMF was very critical about the way Mubarak was running the Egyptian economy. A 1985 IMF study blamed Egypt for being overreliant on foreign aid and recommended that the government raise the price of food and other necessities—even though raising those prices would add yet another burden on the poor.

In 1988, Mubarak favored a slow approach to cutting subsidies and making other changes. He said the IMF acted like a "quack doctor" who orders the patient to take "a huge dose of medicine in one go instead of a daily pill." Showing his frustration, Mubarak said, "The IMF plan aims at killing the Egyptian citizen and is impossible to implement." Nevertheless, Mubarak implemented one of the IMF recommendations, which doubled the price of bread at government-run bakeries. Riots broke out, and three people were killed.

In the 1980s, the Egyptian economy was in such a precarious state that it depended largely on American aid and tourism to stay afloat. Yet even these mainstays were threatened in October 1985, when a terrorist incident involving Egypt captured the world's attention. It was the hijacking by Palestinian militants of the Italian cruise ship *Achille Lauro* off the Egyptian coast. A total of 438 people were held hostage and 1 elderly American passenger was killed. After mediation between the hijackers and the Egyptian government, the ship docked in Egypt. On Mubarak's orders, the hijackers were released, but the United States intervened and captured some of them. Relations between Egypt and the United States deteriorated somewhat as a result of the incident, and American tourism in Egypt fell off sharply.

6

Egypt and the United States

The *Achille Lauro* incident made many Americans aware of the close political, economic, and military relationship that had developed between Egypt and the United States in the Sadat and Mubarak years.

After Israel, Egypt is the United States's second largest foreign aid recipient. In 1988, Egypt received $2.3 billion in American aid, the latest installment in a total of $12 billion in U.S. economic aid and $9 billion in U.S. military payments that Egypt had received since 1974.

But Egypt was not always an American client state. During the mid-1950s the United States was irked by Nasser's anti-Israel, pro-Soviet stance and by his support for nationalist movements in black African countries. The U.S. government refused to help Egypt pay for the Aswân High Dam, a huge project on the Nile to provide massive irrigation and

> *Egypt wants it both ways. They want to distance themselves from the United States because of the mood in the Arab world, and they want to insist they are critical to our security to keep our aid going.*
> —WILLIAM QUANDT
> historian

Mubarak addresses the United Nations General Assembly in 1985. By the end of the 1980s, Mubarak had successfully reestablished relations with most of the Muslim world without damaging Egypt's relationship with the United States or abandoning its peace treaty with Israel.

U.S. secretary of state Henry Kissinger with Anwar Sadat in 1977. The U.S.-Egypt pact that they helped forge gave the Americans extensive military rights in Egypt while enabling the Egyptian armed forces to buy vast amounts of U.S.-made weaponry.

hydroelectric power for the nation's backward agriculture and industry. The Soviets stepped in and finished the job, then initiated arms sales to the Nasser government. After a brief warming period in the early 1960s, American-Egyptian relations were severed in the wake of the Six-Day War in 1967.

In 1974, diplomatic relations between Egypt and the United States were reestablished, and after Sadat signed the peace treaty with Israel, the United States rewarded him with a huge commitment for

aid. "I can see the possibility that 10 years from now," Jimmy Carter told Sadat in April 1977, "our ties to you in the economic, military, and political spheres will be just as strong as the ties we now have with Israel."

U.S. politicians and the American public liked Sadat, who by the end of his life had become perhaps the U.S. government's most faithful ally in the Third World. Mubarak, however, would have a different sort of relationship with the Americans. He withdrew Sadat's offer to let the United States use the Ras Banas naval base on the Red Sea. Hermann Frederick Eilts, a former U.S. ambassador to Egypt, described how American government officials first felt about Egypt's new president. "In contrast to Sadat's geniality and general willingness to acquiesce in American proposals, which had come to be expected by U.S. leaders," said Eilts, "Mubarak was seen as demanding, somewhat abrasive, and

U.S. troops participating in the joint Egyptian-American maneuvers known as Bright Star. The large-scale desert warfare exercise was one of several conducted by the United States in Egypt during the early 1980s.

unbending. His critical candor in speaking to U.S. leaders sometimes grated."

Nevertheless, the mutual dependence between the United States and Egypt remained strong. The U.S. embassy in Cairo is the largest American embassy in the world. By 1986, there were 2,000 people working for it, more than half of them attached to the United States Agency for International Development (USAID), a nonmilitary aid program.

From 1980 to 1982, the number of Americans in Egypt doubled, from 5,000 to about 10,000. Many Americans live in the Cairo suburb of Maadi, which, with its neat streets and comfortable homes, looks much like the wealthy section of an American city. It is very different from the poor slums of Cairo, and even more different from the rural villages of the Delta. Many Egyptians have come to resent the American presence.

Egyptians complained about continued American support for Israel. They were also angry because the United States gave Israel money to do whatever it wanted to do. Aid to Egypt came "with strings attached"; American administrators in Egypt decided how funds were spent.

The USAID program in the 1980s was aimed at a variety of projects, including efforts to control Egypt's massive population problems. From 1977 to 1988, Egypt's family planning program received $170 million from the United States and additional amounts from other governments and the World Bank. Still, little progress was made to slow Egypt's explosive population growth. Other U.S. funds went to the Mubarak government to improve sewage, electricity, telephone, and road systems.

From the American point of view, the most important aspect of the United States's relationship with Egypt is military. Throughout the 1980s and into the 1990s, the United States gave Egypt about $1 billion of military aid annually, and American arms corporations have further profited through Egypt's large purchases of U.S.-made military equipment.

Sadat and Mubarak also allowed the U.S. military its largest presence in the Middle East. The first in a series of joint Egyptian-American military exercises, code-named Bright Star, was held in 1980, involving more than 8,000 Egyptian and American troops and bombing runs by 6 U.S. Air Force B-52 bombers. In 1985, the Reagan administration asked Mubarak to join in a U.S. air attack against Libya that was intended to kill the Libyan leader, Muammar Muhammad al-Qaddafi. But Mubarak was not willing to extend the military relationship

> Cutting back [the aid] would have the effect of wrecking the Middle East peace process.
>
> —MARSHALL BROWN
> director of U.S. Agency for International Development

Defense Minister Abd al-Halim Abu Ghazala sits alongside Mubarak in 1988. Abu Ghazala, a favorite of U.S. military officials, is believed to have tipped the Americans off during the 1985 *Achille Lauro* incident, when Mubarak tried to spirit the cruise ship's Palestinian hijackers out of Egypt.

Egyptian investigators examine a possible bloodstain on board the *Achille Lauro* after the release of the hostages and surrender of the hijackers. One passenger, a wheelchair-bound Jewish American, was killed by the terrorists.

with the United States to so radical an extent. Even though Qaddafi's Libya had had several clashes with Egypt, Mubarak rejected President Reagan's offer.

Starting in the mid-1980s, rumors began to arise of a rivalry between Mubarak and his defense minister, Abd al-Halim Abu Ghazala, the man who managed the Egyptian end of the U.S. military aid pipeline. The two men are very different in physical appearance and mannerisms, and many Americans preferred Abu Ghazala, who seemed more anxious to please the United States than did Mubarak. As the political scientist Robert Springborg notes, "The two men are as unlike as chalk and cheese. Abu Ghazala is an articulate, forceful, ambitious figure who impresses those around him. His off-the-record meetings with U.S. reporters, in contrast to those with Mubarak, leave the audience impressed with his grasp of facts and figures, receptivity to ideas, and ability to address points directly and concisely. Whereas Mubarak is a man who gives the impression of having had the presidency thrust upon him and having out of a sense of duty resolved to do the best job possible, Abu Ghazala gives every sign of thirsting for the position and wanting to use it to put a program into effect."

One of the most visible clashes between Mubarak and Abu Ghazala occurred during the October 1985 *Achille Lauro* affair, an incident that originated in events involving the United States and Israel. A few days before the hijacking, Israeli air force jets bombed the headquarters of the Palestine Liberation Organization (PLO), south of Tunis, the capital of Tunisia. The raid, generally believed to have been supported by U.S. president Reagan, left 69 Palestinians and Tunisians dead. The four Palestinian hijackers of the *Achille Lauro* said they were acting out of retaliation for the Tunis air raid.

After the hijackers agreed to surrender to the Egyptian government, Mubarak did not want to turn them over to U.S. authorities; to hand them over to the United States, he knew, would alienate most of the Arab world and dash any hope of repairing Egyptian relations with other Arab governments. So Mubarak tried a bluff.

Egypt took the four Palestinians into custody at

In the immediate aftermath of Sadat's assassination the contrast [between Abu Ghazala and Mubarak] was highlighted before world television audiences. Abu Ghazala stood erect, pointing his baton at the fleeing assassins and yelling orders to give chase. Mubarak had crawled under chairs and was extricated by bodyguards who bundled him away unceremoniously.
—ROBERT SPRINGBORG
Middle East historian

Mubarak, in a rare public display of anger, denounces the United States for forcing down an Egyptian jetliner carrying the *Achille Lauro* hijackers to political asylum in Tunisia. The captured terrorists were taken instead to Italy to face charges of piracy and murder.

the Egyptian coastal city of Port Said. The hostages and crew of the *Achille Lauro* were allowed to leave the ship. Mubarak then announced that the hijackers had already left the country. But in reality they were still being held in Egypt; only later, according to Mubarak's plan, would they be secretly flown to Tunisia, where the PLO would determine their fate. Meanwhile, U.S. intelligence officials were secretly monitoring Mubarak's telephone calls. In one of his conversations on that hectic day, Mubarak revealed

the flight number of the Egyptian plane that would take the hijackers out of Egypt.

Mubarak's phone conversations were being monitored by President Ronald Reagan's national security adviser, John Poindexter, and his aide, Colonel Oliver North. According to the American journalist Bob Woodward, North came up with a plan to intercept the Egyptian plane carrying the hijackers and force it to land. Reagan approved North's plan.

The Egyptian jetliner carrying the Palestinian hijackers, a PLO mediator, and an Egyptian crew took off from Cairo on October 10 and was closely monitored by American military intelligence. Four U.S. Navy F-14 fighter jets took off from the deck of an American aircraft carrier stationed in the Mediterranean Sea, caught up with the Egyptian airliner, and forced it to land in Sicily. When the plane touched down, the four Palestinians were arrested by Italian police and charged with murder and kidnapping.

Angry Cairenes burn a U.S. flag during a 1985 demonstration protesting an Israeli air raid against the Palestine Liberation Organization (PLO) headquarters in Tunisia. Israeli raids and incursions against various Arab states throughout the 1980s forced Mubarak to strike a delicate balance between support and condemnation of Israel and the United States.

Mubarak called the American action "an act of piracy" and a "stab in the back." As a new wave of anti-American feeling rolled across Egypt, he called on the United States to apologize. Transcripts of Mubarak's phone calls revealed that Mubarak had called U.S. secretary of state George Shultz "crazy" for thinking that Egypt would turn over the four Palestinians to the United States.

But according to the French newspaper *Le Monde*, Abu Ghazala revealed to the Americans the flight number of the plane carrying the Palestinian

Mubarak acknowledges the cheers of the Egyptian parliament at the start of his second term in 1987. That same year 11 Arab states renewed diplomatic relations with Egypt.

hijackers. This report, which the Egyptian government officially denied, widened the rift between Mubarak and Abu Ghazala. It widened still further one month later when Abu Ghazala was blamed for planning the botched Egyptian rescue mission in Malta. A few days later Mubarak tried to boot the defense minister upstairs by offering him the vice-presidency. Abu Ghazala said he would accept, but only if he could also keep his job at the Defense Ministry. Only Abu Ghazala's successful crushing of the CSF revolt in February 1986 enabled him to keep his job.

With Abu Ghazala's position safe and the Americans confident that their man would remain defense minister, American-Egyptian relations soon returned to normal. Reagan sent a conciliatory letter to Mubarak, and John Whitehead, a senior official from the U.S. State Department, visited Mubarak to smooth over hurt feelings.

By the end of the 1980s, Egypt's relationship as a client of the United States had been fully restored. With it, however, came a renewal of Egyptian anxieties that the sheer size of the U.S. aid program had created, in the words of one Cairo magazine, an "American shadow government in Egypt serving as a tool of American penetration." As one Egyptian official put it, "We are becoming more dependent when we were supposed to become more self-reliant."

7

Egypt, the Arabs, and Israel

Egypt's relationship with the United States is very closely tied to its relationship with Israel, and that has been the case from the moment Sadat signed the Camp David accords. Mubarak continued the peace with Israel, despite the ardent opposition and even ostracism of the rest of the Muslim world. During a speech on December 23, 1981, in his second full month in power, Hosni Mubarak outlined his commitment to the treaty with Israel:

> We chose this to be a proud peace, one which will achieve for us, for our Arab brothers, and for all states and of the area what the wars of the last 25 years failed to achieve: stability and coexistence. It is a peace that all parties will adopt, out of conviction and sincerity, as a way of life and behavior; a peace that is built on the sincere adherence to international law and human rights. This is the peace that we strive to achieve as we continue on this strenuous path that we are determined to follow.

Mubarak is embraced by PLO leader Yasir Arafat in 1986. Mubarak's support for direct negotiations between the PLO and Israel, which the Israeli government sternly opposed throughout the 1980s, led to a chilling of relations between Egypt and Israel as the decade wore on.

In March 1982, Mubarak again said he would not change the peace policy: "We are not going to change anything. . . . We have sacrificed a lot for peace. We don't intend to overthrow it. We are looking forward to much better relations with Israel." Mubarak's comments were a relief to some American and Israeli officials, who at first did not believe that Mubarak would stick to the terms of the peace treaty.

However much the treaty with Israel profited Egypt in terms of peaceful coexistence and monetary gain, it also cost Egypt enormously. Many Muslims, both at home and abroad, believed that Egypt —and by extension, Mubarak—was a traitor, selling out the cause of Arab unity and the Palestinian people in exchange for American dollars. It was vital for Mubarak to overturn this image, and he set out to do so with his characteristic efficiency and quiet determination.

That approach contrasted sharply with that of Sadat, who on one occasion referred to King Fahd of Saudi Arabia as a "donkey" and the other leaders of the Arab world as "dwarfs." Mubarak, on the other hand, was conciliatory in his public utterances about his fellow Arab leaders and stressed his country's place in the Arab community. "Egypt is a part of the Arab nation," said Mubarak in a November 1983 speech to the Egyptian parliament. "It does not split from the Arab nation, nor does it forsake the Arab nation's causes. Egypt's Arabism is not a garment we wear when we want, nor can anyone remove it from us."

Mubarak's first step in repairing Egypt's links to the Arab world was his declaration of support for Iraq, an Arab nation, in its war against Iran, a non-Arab nation. The Iran-Iraq War (also known as the Persian Gulf War) had been raging since 1980, and soon after he became president, Mubarak decided to sell arms and ammunition to the Iraqis. Mubarak also hinted that Egypt was ready to join the Iraqis on the battlefield if the Iranians threatened to win the war—a potent hint in light of the fact that Egypt has the largest army in the Arab world. Thousands of Egyptians did indeed fight alongside Iraqi soldiers. By 1984, Egypt was providing Iraq with $1 billion worth of arms and ammunition annually. Mubarak's extensive support for Iraq helped diminish much of the ill will that other Arab nations felt toward Egypt for its treaty with Israel.

The warming process was slow. In 1982, Mubarak visited Saudi Arabia, another Middle Eastern ally of the United States that was heavily dependent on American weapons. On that same visit he met with Yasir Arafat, head of the PLO. In late December 1983, Mubarak and Arafat met again, this time in Cairo. It marked the first visit to Egypt by an Arab leader since relations were broken during Sadat's presidency.

While the meeting was hailed in the Arab world, the Israelis were none too pleased with Arafat's show of friendship for Mubarak. The Israeli government, claiming that the meeting violated the Egyptian-Israeli peace agreement, called it "a severe blow to the peace process in the Middle East."

In January 1984, Egypt accepted an invitation to resume its membership in the Islamic Conference Organization (ICO). Nine months later, Jordan resumed formal diplomatic ties with Egypt. Jordanian officials told a U.S. newspaper that their country had reestablished relations because Mubarak had cleansed Egypt of Sadat's legacy.

"All over the Arab world now people say, 'Egypt, Egypt,' " Mubarak exulted in the afterglow of his nation's 1984 diplomatic success. "Egypt is the leader, the biggest nation of the Arab world, the nation that can influence the situation more than any other. Everywhere, every day you hear the voices, 'Egypt should return, Egypt should return.' " Even though a large-scale diplomatic breakthrough with Egypt's Arab brethren was still three years away, Egypt, with its professionals, laborers, and other citizens holding jobs all over the Middle East, had reforged extensive links with the rest of the Arab world.

Mubarak hoped that the big breakthrough would come in early November 1987, when Middle Eastern leaders met at the conference of the Arab League in

Mubarak with Libyan leader Colonel Muammar al-Qaddafi in 1989, prior to talks that ended 12 years of hostility marked by violent border clashes and a stream of acrimonious rhetoric.

Amman, Jordan. The national leaders and top government officials assembled at the conference voted to allow any Arab nation to resume diplomatic relations with Egypt. Such a decision was "a sovereign matter to be decided by each state in accordance with its constitution and laws." Nevertheless, Egypt was not yet allowed to rejoin the Arab League.

After the conference ended, nine Arab states, most of them considered "moderate" in their views on the United States, resumed official diplomatic relations with Egypt: the United Arab Emirates, Kuwait, Iraq, Bahrain, Qatar, the Arab Republic of Yemen, Saudi Arabia, Morocco, and Mauritania.

Several weeks later, Tunisia and South Yemen re-established formal ties with Egypt. By 1989, the only Arab states without diplomatic relations with Egypt were Lebanon, Libya, and Syria.

Libya and Syria remained implacable foes of Mubarak. Through the 1980s and into the 1990s, Syria's president, Hafez al-Assad, called for Egypt to reject the peace treaty with Israel. There was some irony to Assad's dispute with Mubarak. Both had been fighter pilots; the two men had even flown together as young trainees. In the late 1980s, Assad said that he and Mubarak were on "good terms" and that "we speak the same language, the language of pilots." The friendly personal relationship between the two leaders has kept the Egypt-Syria dispute on relatively cordial terms.

The same cannot be said about the relationship between Mubarak and Qaddafi (in 1984, for example, Mubarak called Qaddafi "mad") or about the dispute between Egypt and Libya. The ill will between the two countries stretches back to July 1977, when Egypt and Libya fought a short but violent border war that came close to erupting again in 1981. Shortly thereafter, Libya threatened to attack Sudan, Egypt's neighbor to the south. Mubarak vowed to intervene militarily to protect Sudan, and Qaddafi backed down. Then in the summer of 1984, Libya was accused of laying mines in the waters of the Red Sea near the Suez Canal shipping lanes, and there were even rumors that Libya was planning to bomb Egypt's Aswân High Dam. A month later Mubarak warned Qaddafi that aggressive actions against Egypt would be like "playing with fire." After that tensions between the two nations dissipated somewhat.

By the late 1980s, Egypt had regained a prominent place in the Arab world. But there were still those who deeply resented Mubarak's relationship with the United States—and with Israel.

From the moment he took office, Mubarak kept to the letter of Sadat's peace agreement with the Israelis. But he did not expand the new relationship between the two nations. By the end of the 1980s, political analysts were calling the Egyptian-Israeli relationship a "cold peace." But despite the chilly feelings between the two countries, the fact remains that the cycle of Egyptian-Israeli wars was finally broken.

Israel completed its withdrawal from the Sinai, as stipulated by the treaty, in April 1982 (Israeli troops had to forcibly remove a group of militant Israeli settlers in order to complete the operation on time). Mubarak applauded the withdrawal as a "magnificent achievement," adding that the "people of Israel have shown an enthusiasm for peace." But then he went on to list some of the grievances Egypt still had against Israel. "The building of new Israeli establishments in various parts of the West Bank and Gaza Strip," he said, "leads to more suspicion and makes the hopes of the future wane."

There was another bone of contention between the two countries. In returning the Sinai, the Israelis failed to return to Egyptian sovereignty a tiny strip of land called Taba on the east coast of the Sinai Peninsula, 1 of 15 points of dispute over where exactly the border between the 2 countries was actually situated. Taba, a 700-yard-long strip of beach, was the largest of these disputed points. And what made the struggle over its ownership so bitter was the luxury beachfront hotel that an Israeli entrepreneur had built on the plot of land.

The Israelis claimed that Taba was theirs and should remain under their control; the Egyptians disagreed and maintained that it should be returned with the rest of the Sinai. The Mubarak government noted that Israel returned Taba to Egyptian control after the Suez War; how, they asked, could Taba be considered part of the Sinai in 1956 but not in 1982?

Part of the problem could be traced to inaccurate mapmaking. In 1906, a British surveyor charted the border between what was then the Ottoman territory of Palestine and British-controlled Egypt. When he drew in the border, he used a very thick pencil on a small-scale map. The result was that the width of his pencil line turned out to be the same as the width of Taba on the map. Israel claimed its border reached to the southern edge of the line, Egypt the northern side. The Taba affair would drag on for four years before the countries agreed to submit the case to international arbitration. Finally, in 1986, the strip of land was awarded to Egypt.

Although the Egyptians got the Sinai back, other key provisions of the Camp David process did not come off as planned. The accords called for a series of Egyptian-Israeli talks to discuss the possibility of Palestinian self-rule in the Israeli-occupied territories of Gaza and the West Bank. The United States government vaguely agreed to "full autonomy" for

In the hot sea breeze the "cold peace" between the two nations seemed to warm—but only a few degrees.
—DIANE TURNBULL journalist, *Newsweek*, referring to the scene at the turning over of Taba to Egypt

the Palestinians, but the Israelis refused to make such a pledge. The autonomy talks lasted from August 1979 to June 1982, but Israel did not change its position. The talks were abandoned.

In June 1982, Israel invaded Lebanon. The invasion was intended to destroy the PLO, the largest group in the Palestinian nationalist movement. Outraged Egyptian opposition groups staged large demonstrations against Israel and the United States and demanded a break in Egyptian-Israeli ties, but the Mubarak government held firm. Syrian newspapers went so far as to blame the war on Egypt by claiming that the Camp David accords had allowed the Israelis to move their troops from the Egyptian border to the Lebanese border.

In September 1982, Lebanese Christian forces allied with the Israeli occupation force massacred hundreds of Palestinian Arab civilians in two refugee camps in Beirut. This prompted Mubarak to finally speak out against the Israeli invasion. He publicly called on the Israeli army to withdraw from Lebanon and recalled Egypt's ambassador from Tel Aviv in protest.

The Lebanon war was a serious blow to Egypt's relationship with Israel. As one Egyptian official noted, "That adventure destroyed five years of work. . . . Because of this aggression we are back to square one on the whole process of peace in the Middle East." Many of the planned Egyptian-Israeli cultural and economic exchanges were promptly abandoned. Egyptian import and export licenses with Israel were canceled and the Israeli tourism office in Cairo was closed.

In October 1985, Egyptian-Israeli relations deteriorated further when an Egyptian border guard named Suleiman Khater went berserk, shooting and killing seven Israeli tourists in the Sinai. Khater was arrested by Egyptian police and later found dead in his prison cell. The government claimed he had committed suicide, but many Egyptians believed he had been killed by the police. Khater became a folk hero for Egyptian opposition groups who believed his actions were in revenge for a previous Israeli air raid on the Tunis headquarters of

Mubarak casts his ballot in the 1987 parliamentary elections. Although he implemented free elections at the parliamentary level in the 1980s, the presidential election remained little more than a rubber stamp for Mubarak.

the PLO. Large demonstrations were held in Cairo to honor Khater, who was called a martyr to the Arab cause. Israeli feelings were not soothed when Mubarak called the incident a "minor affair."

In September 1986, five years after the last Egyptian-Israeli summit, Mubarak and Israeli prime minister Shimon Peres met at a conference in Alexandria, Egypt. Peres, the most moderate premier Israel had had in more than a decade, was about to step down from the post. It was at this meeting that Egypt and Israel agreed to submit the Taba issue to international arbitration. Mubarak restored full diplomatic relations with Israel.

But the cold peace endured as the 1990s got under way. Egypt remains adamantly opposed to Israel's annexation of East Jerusalem and its continued policy of encouraging Jewish settlement in the East Bank. Whereas Sadat had visited Israel three times as president, including a visit to Jerusalem on his first trip, as of 1990, Mubarak had still never visited Israel and had turned down repeated Israeli invitations. Once, however, Mubarak almost made the trip; in March 1982, before the return of the Sinai, he was scheduled to fly to Tel Aviv. But when the Israeli prime minister, Menachem Begin, insisted that the trip include a stop in East Jerusalem, Mubarak canceled. That was as close to setting foot in Israel as Mubarak had ever come.

Egypt came a long way under Mubarak in the first nine years of his rule. Friendly relations with the rest of the Arab world were reestablished without sacrificing the enormous amount of American aid to keep the economy afloat. Continuing improvements in sewer, water, electricity, telephone, and transportation systems — including a French-built subway opened in 1987 — helped Cairo cope with its mushrooming population.

But the Egyptian population, expected to reach 80 million by the year 2000, remained the nation's most intractable problem. Many observers wondered how an already strained country, with less and less farmland and ever more crowded city slums, could cope with all the people. The job market grew tighter and tighter, with the safety valve

> *The essence of the peace treaty between Egypt and Israel has been respected by both sides, but the full promise of peace and normal relations has not been achieved.*
>
> —WILLIAM QUANDT
> historian

of employment in rich Arab countries lost because of the worldwide decline in the oil business. Would the frustrations of such a dim economic future lead to great, even violent, social upheaval?

The previous solution to such problems — borrowing money from the IMF, World Bank, or foreign governments — had already been exposed as a failure. Nevertheless, it was the only short-term solution available. In 1987, with Egypt's foreign debt standing at nearly $40 billion, Mubarak agreed to IMF demands to cut government subsidies to the nation's poor. In return, Egypt was allowed to put off paying back loans from the United States, West Germany, Japan, and Sweden. But Egypt's economic troubles worsened. With inflation surpassing 25 percent in 1990 and the government still at the mercy of the IMF and its strict economic orders, life for Egypt's poor became increasingly difficult.

Mubarak faced a continuing challenge from Egypt's Islamic fundamentalists as the new decade dawned. In 1988, in the midst of renewed fundamentalist activity, the government extended the state of emergency that had existed since the day of Sadat's assassination and arrested hundreds of religious activists. The Mubarak government then began investigating business dealings by Islamic investment companies, which were popular among the Egyptian middle class. Government investigators ruled that the companies were being mismanaged, and the police took into custody the founder of one of the large investment houses. Many Egyptians charged that the investigation was nothing more than government harassment of the Islamic firms.

Though the Washington-Cairo aid pipeline operated smoothly throughout the 1980s, a 1988 dispute briefly threatened to disrupt the flow. In June of that year, U.S. law enforcement officials charged three Egyptian officials and three Americans with trying to smuggle carbon-carbon, a key substance in the construction of American missiles. According to the *Washington Post*, Egypt's defense minister, Abu Ghazala, was involved in the plot.

By the late 1980s, Camp David had become an-

> *The Egyptian president is always concerned about being isolated in the Arab world, since he is the only Arab leader who talks regularly to the Israelis.*
> —W. E. SMITH
> journalist, *Time*

In a March 1989 ceremony, Egyptian army officers salute the raising of their national flag over Taba, a strip of land claimed by both Egypt and Israel. After a seven-year dispute in which Mubarak and successive Israeli premiers showed admirable restraint, an international arbitrator awarded Taba and its luxury hotel (seen in background) to Egypt.

other word for "failure" in the search for peace in the Middle East, but Mubarak tried to keep his role as peacemaker. In 1988, he convinced PLO leader Yasir Arafat to moderate his stance on Israel. Arafat publicly renounced terrorism and recognized Israel's right to exist. As a result, on December 14, 1988, the United States said it would open a "diplomatic dialogue" with the PLO. Mubarak claimed it was he who convinced U.S. secretary of state George Shultz to enter into the talks. Later in December 1988, Mubarak tried to get the PLO and Israel to negotiate directly; he even added that he, like Sadat, would visit Israel if it would help bring peace. "If the visit will lead to a solution of the Palestinian problem and to the realization of a just peace," said Mubarak, "I am ready." But Israel refused to negotiate with the PLO, and the trip never came off.

Some Egyptians at the start of the 1990s believed that Mubarak had not moved effectively to solve many of the country's problems. They still looked back to the days of the charismatic Nasser, when Egypt spearheaded the Arab nationalist movement. As one Egyptian put it, "Mubarak hasn't done anything wrong. But then again, he hasn't done anything." Mubarak's supporters answered the criticism by pointing out that Mubarak "likes to go step by step," as a member of Egypt's parliament put it.

Whichever is true, Mubarak looked forward to his second decade in office — and beyond that, Egypt's place in the 21st century — with characteristic deliberation. "It is our generation's fate to bear things," he said in a 1989 speech, "and there is no escape from that. We bear as much as we can, to build a better future for our children."

Further Reading

Al-Sayyid Marsot, Afaf Lutfi. *A Short History of Modern Egypt.* Cambridge, England: Cambridge University Press, 1985.

Amdur, Richard. *Menachem Begin.* New York: Chelsea House, 1988.

Atherton, Alfred Leroy, Jr. *Egypt and U.S. Interests.* Washington, DC: Johns Hopkins University Press, 1988.

Aufderheide, Patricia. *Anwar Sadat.* New York: Chelsea House, 1985.

Burns, William J. *Economic Aid and American Policy Toward Egypt, 1955–1981.* Albany: State University of New York Press, 1985.

DeChancie, John. *Gamal Abdel Nasser.* New York: Chelsea House, 1988.

Hasou, Tawfig Y. *The Struggle for the Arab World.* London: KPI, 1985.

Heikal, Mohamed. *Autumn of Fury: The Assassination of Sadat.* New York: Random House, 1983.

Herzog, Chaim. *The Arab-Israeli Wars: War and Peace in the Middle East.* New York: Random House, 1982.

Hopwood, Derek. *Egypt, Politics and Society, 1945–1981.* Boston: Allen and Unwin, 1982.

Kepel, Gilles. *Muslim Extremism in Egypt, The Prophet and the Pharaoh.* Berkeley: University of California Press, 1985.

Lippman, Thomas W. *Egypt After Nasser: Sadat, Peace and the Mirage of Prosperity.* New York: Paragon House, 1989.

McDermott, Anthony. *Egypt From Nasser to Mubarak: A Flawed Revolution.* New York: Routledge, Chapman & Hall, 1988.

Neff, Donald. *Warriors at Suez: Eisenhower Takes America into the Middle East.* New York: The Linden Press/Simon & Schuster, 1981.

Springborg, Robert. *Mubarak's Egypt: Fragmentation of the Political Order.* Boulder, CO: Westview Press, 1989.

Stefoff, Rebecca. *Yasir Arafat.* New York: Chelsea House, 1988.

Quandt, William B. *Camp David: Peacemaking and Politics.* Washington, DC: Brookings Institution, 1986.

———. *The Middle East: Ten Years After Camp David.* Washington, DC: Brookings Institution, 1988.

Vail, John J. *David Ben-Gurion.* New York: Chelsea House, 1987.

Vatikiotis, P. J. *Nasser and His Generation.* New York: St. Martin's Press, 1978.

Waterbury, John. *The Egypt of Nasser and Sadat: The Political Economy of Two Regimes.* Princeton, NJ: Princeton University Press, 1983.

Chronology

May 4, 1929	Born Muhammad Hosni Mubarak in Kafr-el-Meselha, Egypt
Nov. 1947	Enters Egyptian Military Academy and later, Egyptian Air Academy
May 14, 1948	Israeli independence declared; Palestine War, also known as Israeli War of Independence, begins next day
Feb. 1949	Egypt and Israel sign peace agreement
1952	Mubarak becomes pilot instructor; King Farouk deposed
June 18, 1953	Egyptian republic declared
1956	Nasser announces nationalization of the Suez Canal (July); Israeli troops invade Sinai; British and French move against the canal (Oct.)
1958	Mubarak marries Suzanne Sabet
1964–65	Takes military training course in the Soviet Union
June 1967	Six-Day War from June 5–11; Israel defeats Egypt, Jordan, Iraq, and Syria, capturing Sinai, Gaza Strip, West Bank, and Golan Heights
1970	Nasser dies; Sadat named president
1972	Mubarak appointed commander in chief of the air force and deputy minister of war
Oct. 1973	Egypt and Syria fight Israel to a deadlock in 18-day Ramadan War, also known as Yom Kippur War; elements of Egyptian army cross Suez Canal into Sinai
April 1975	Sadat appoints Mubarak vice-president
Nov. 1977	Sadat visits Israel
Sept. 1978	Sadat, Begin, and Carter sign the Camp David accords in Washington, D.C.
Nov. 1978	Egypt voted out of Arab League
Oct. 1981	Sadat assassinated; Mubarak, the lone candidate, elected president
April 1982	Israel completes withdrawal from Sinai
June 1982	Israel invades Lebanon
Sept. 1982	Mubarak recalls Egyptian ambassador to Israel
1986	Central Security Forces revolt; Mubarak and Israeli prime minister Peres meet in Alexandria; Mubarak restores full diplomatic relations with Israel
1987	Elected to second term as president; 11 Arab states resume diplomatic relations with Egypt
March 1989	Israel returns Taba to Egypt

Index

John Solecki holds a master's degree from the Columbia University School of International Affairs and a certificate from Columbia University's Middle East Institute. The author of numerous articles on Arab politics and U.S. policy-making in the Middle East, he studied Arabic in Cairo, Egypt, in 1983, has traveled extensively throughout the Arab world, and is currently living and working in Saudi Arabia.

Arthur M. Schlesinger, jr., taught history at Harvard for many years and is currently Albert Schweitzer Professor of the Humanities at City University of New York. He is the author of numerous highly praised works in American history and has twice been awarded the Pulitzer Prize. He served in the White House as special assistant to Presidents Kennedy and Johnson.